The *Art* of Teaching Adults

photo: Galiano Photography

About the Author

Peter Renner grew up in Germany and, at age thirteen, began a five-year apprenticeship to become an innkeeper. His journeyman travels took him to England, Sweden, Wales, the United States, and Canada – there to first become a college instructor, later an educational consultant and textbook author. Curiosity led him to study in London, Vancouver, and Oxford, obtaining degrees in hotel management, counseling, adult education, and curriculum development. Now in the second half of life, he lives on a small island off the West coast, practicing *la dolce far niente* – the sweet art of being idle .

The *Art* of Teaching Adults

How to become an exceptional instructor & facilitator

Peter Renner

Training Associates, Vancouver

The publisher acknowledges the generous permission given to use the previously copy-righted material on pages 41-47 by Training House, Inc., Post Office Box 3090, Princeton, NJ 08543; telephone (609) 452-1505; fax (609) 243-9368.

American and Canadian CIP data available upon request
ISBN 0-9690465-9-6 (cloth)
ISBN 0-9697319-0-6 (paper)

Edited by Elaine Jones
Designed by George Vaitkunas
Typeset in Stone Serif and Stone Sans
Proofread by Trish Letient
Printed by Hignell Printing Limited

First printing July 1993
Second printing August 1994
Third printing July 1995
Fourth printing May 1996
Fifth printing September 1997

Training Associates
Suite 720, 999 West Broadway
Vancouver, BC V5Z 1K5 Canada
Telephone (604) 732-4552 Fax (604) 738-4080

For Karen
loving, giving, enduring
in memoriam

&

For Herman
in celebration of thirty years
of unconditional friendship

*It is the supreme art of the teacher
to awaken joy in creative
expression and knowledge.*

– Albert Einstein
Motto for the Astronomy Building
Junior College, Pasadena, California.

Acknowledgement

The Art of Teaching Adults is a revised and expanded version of the venerable *Instructor's Survival Kit.* That book sold close to 50,000 copies and, during its ten-year life, established an underground reputation on three continents.

I am thankful to Dawn Saintsbury Glyckherr for kickstarting the dreaded process of writing this book. She interviewed a focus group of adult educators scattered across several time zones, from British Columbia to Puerto Rico. Each offered ideas and encouragement, helping me decide what to keep, what to add, and what to delete. My gratitude goes to Sandy Barabé, Carey Conway, Jean Dalton, Diane Donaldson, Inés González, Doug Hone, Doug Kerr, Toni Lashbrook, David L'Heureux, Penny Reid, Mary Speller, Dixie Stockmayer, Doug Taylor, Veronica Timmons, and Mardy Wheeler. Scott Parry generously offered an article on "handling questions."

Elaine Jones edited the manuscript through many rewrites and, with firm and gentle directions, transformed my enthusiastic ramblings into a coherent text. George Vaitkunas expertly embraced the challenge of type selection, page layout, and cover design. Their attention to detail and high standards of professionalism are an inspiration to me.

Peter Renner
Galiano Island

Please Write in this Book

If you bought it, it's yours. Why not get the most from it?

Reading and paying attention are of course important to learning. But remember, what's in these pages comes from someone else ... not from you. True learning and significant growth come only when you take up the ideas, play with them, experiment, test their validity. So, add your personal comments, your questions, your ideas for the next course you'll be teaching. If you disagree with what you read, make a note of it: write it in the margins or paste over top of what's there. Let this book reflect your thoughts, beliefs, and actions. Then watch what happens the next time you read the same passage. Bon Voyage!

Contents

1 On becoming a teacher

To teach a teacher
ill beseemeth me.

– William Shakespeare,
  Love's Labour Lost, Act II,
  Scene 1.

You and I are on a common path – we both want to become the best teachers we can be. I hope this book can assist you in your pursuit. It contains a variety of information, from the most practical aspects of the classroom – room setups, flip charts, lesson planning – to techniques which can create agreeable learning climates, acknowledge participants' individuality, and help them to come to grips with a given subject.

But before you read on, I'd like to tell you how I came by the assumptions and beliefs that now guide my behavior in the classroom and, by extension, serve as a theoretical backdrop for *The Art of Teaching Adults*. Perhaps you'll find them useful in developing your own working theory.

Traditional roles

By its very structure, classroom-based instruction assumes that all students learn more or less in the same manner and at the same pace. Traditionally, the teacher's role has been to cover the material through verbal communication and written texts. When I began teaching in the early seventies, one of my first professors defined adult education as "a relationship between an educational agent and a learner in which the agent selects, arranges, and continually directs a sequence of progressive tasks that provide systematic experiences to achieve learning."[1] Accordingly, I set out to acquire the skills necessary to be such an agent: I learned how to design courses, write learning objectives, draw up lesson plans, present lectures, select written materials, use the overhead projector, guide discussions, give quizzes, and evaluate my courses.

Teacher-centered and learner-centered instruction

However, I soon became dissatisfied with my adopted role definition. Most of what occurred in my classroom was initiated by me and conducted at my pace. The harder I worked at organizing and presenting, and the more I prepared and studied, the less my students shared my enthusiasm. By trying to be the best educational agent under the sun, my instruction had become oppressively *teacher-centered*.

Further readings led me to the works of John Dewey, the early twentieth-century American educator. To him, a teacher either overrides the learners' interests and replaces them by ideas and goals prescribed by others, or attempts to bring out each learner's potential competencies. Dewey favored the latter and proposed a *learner-centered* approach, which focuses on the students' analysis of their experiences and encourages them to become increasingly self-directed and responsible for their own learning. Under such a regime, skills are acquired through activities that the learners, with the help of the teacher, employ to serve their interests and needs. First-hand and vicarious experiences, dialogue among learners and between teachers and learners, and thoughtful analysis and interpretation become the focus of instruction.[2]

Seeking balance

Ready to abandon formal tuition, I prepared for my next class. Out with lectures and old habits was my battle cry; in with small groups, case studies, role-playing, individual assignments, team projects, and learning journals. But my students were utterly unprepared; after years of teacher-centered conditioning, they did not respond well to what I had to offer. Fortunately, they were generous and helped me to learn while we all adjusted to a new way of learning. Later I reread Dewey and found his advice to *combine* my "traditional" function, that of transmitter of accumulated wisdom, with my "new" function, that of learning facilitator.

The time being the seventies, I also encountered Paulo Freire, the passionate critic from Latin America. Like Dewey, he deplored the dependency relationship that often develops between teacher and learners. He wrote of "narration sickness," wherein the teacher monopolizes the majority of air time, and described as "banking education" the preoccupation with filling students with facts and beliefs, expecting such "deposits" to be filed, stored, and accounted for on demand. If I wanted to help students become inquirers and thinkers about themselves and their environment, Freire advised, I needed to view them as partners in the instructional process and myself as a colearner. Freire recommended a new "problem-posing" education in which learners and teachers jointly address issues of importance to them, sharing the roles and functions of learner and teacher.[3]

Purposeful instruction

It didn't take me long to realize that there was more to teaching than knowing my subject and experimenting with techniques: I came to view my role in the context of my learners' total experience *and* to see myself as a learner as well. Not unlike myself, participants bring unique attitudes, interests, and abilities; each comes for different reasons, and with separate expectations. As a facilitator, my task was to devise learning opportunities that would enable individuals to meet

When in deep water, become a diver.

– Ralph Blum,
The Book of Runes.

their specific learning needs. And we would have to meet the needs of the organization that brought us together.

Experiential learning

At this juncture, the writings of Kurt Lewin, Carl Rogers, and Malcolm Knowles began to influence my work. Lewin's work has had a profound impact on American social psychology and organizational behavior; I first heard of him as the principal creator of *T-groups,* a problem-solving process called *force-field analysis*, and the concept of *feedback* borrowed from electrical engineering. His observations of groups showed the value of interpersonal communication for learning and changes in behavior. He advocated the establishment of learning environments in which participants had a sense of belonging, security, and freedom to make choices. Necessary ingredients should extend to "voluntary attendance, informality of meetings, freedom of expression, and avoidance of pressure...."[4] Learning, change, and personal growth, according to Lewin's Experiential Learning Model, are facilitated best by a process that begins with an experience followed by the collection of observations about that experience. This information is then analyzed and the resulting conclusion used by the learners to modify their behavior and select new experiences.[5]

The process of facilitation

To know how to suggest is the great art of teaching.

– Henri-Frédéric Amiel (1828-1881), Swiss philosopher-critic.

Carl Rogers has made important contributions to counseling and adult education. Arising from his client-centered therapy, a learner-centered approach invites learners to take full responsibility for decisions, actions, and consequences. The teacher's task is to be accepting, supportive, and empathetic – establishing a pattern of communication that creates a climate of trust and safety. The teacher becomes a coinquirer and colearner and makes available a wide range of resources and learning techniques. The learner, in turn, is encouraged to take risks, experiment, and confront issues and problems that may have inhibited learning. The educator, likewise, develops a new measure of "genuineness"– the ability to take risks by being honest, admitting personal biases, expressing hopes, and sharing concerns. Above all, the emphasis remains focused on the learner's goals and aspirations.[6]

The adult learner

Malcolm Knowles's contribution is centered on his concept of "andragogy," a learning theory for adults distinct from "pedagogy," one concerning children. Four concepts give a taste of Knowles's work.

• *Changes in self-concept.* As we grow and mature, our self-concept moves from total dependency (the reality of the infant) to increasing self-directedness.

- *The role of experience.* We accumulate an expanding reservoir of experiences that are a rich resource and provide a base for new learning. Teaching techniques that involve practice, reflection, and analysis (discussion, simulation, case study, field experience, and role-play) are particularly appropriate.
- *Readiness to learn.* Adults are less motivated by biological development and academic pressure than by the tasks related to social roles. Rather than presenting what *ought* to be learned, the teacher offers choices to enable students to concentrate on what is important at a particular point in their development.
- *Orientation to learning.* If children are subject-oriented in their learning, Knowles argued, then adults tend to be problem-focused. They come to the classroom because of some gaps in their knowledge; they want information and skills that can be applied in the real world now.[7]

Gimme structure!

By now I experienced a new set of learning needs: how should I organize the *content* of my courses? While I had developed a certain style regarding *process*, I was confused about ways of structuring course content. Regardless of who spells it out – the sponsoring organization, the learners, or the teacher as subject-matter expert – each educational event is centered around a body of knowledge, which needs to be arranged in some way. In my search for ideas, I turned from the humanists to the behaviorists and found much-needed advice in the writings of B.F. Skinner, Robert Mager, and Jerrold Kemp.

I met B.F. Skinner's work with much resistance; by reputation, his theories run counter to my humanist image of learners as autonomous beings capable of self-actualization. To Skinner, learning occurs not because behavior has been stimulated (by some inner drive, say, or the teacher's input), but because it is *reinforced*: behavior is determined by its consequences. Luckily, I found a summer course on "behavior modification," by a professor who taught like a humanist. Through him I discovered just how much of Skinner's viewpoint agreed with, or confirmed, the humanist ideas I had recently put into practice. Here are just a few Skinnerian gems which easily fit into the evolving puzzle.

- Behavior that is rewarded is more likely to occur again. Example: Teacher nods, smiles, or similarly rewards a participant's contribution during a discussion.
- Behavior that goes unreinforced is eventually extinguished. Example: Teacher or group members repeatedly ignore contributions made by a participant.
- Letting learners know that they have modified their behavior toward a desired outcome serves as a reinforcement. Examples: The group

applauds spontaneously at the end of a member's presentation; the teacher adds a written comment in a learner's journal: "Your observations are becoming more concise."

- When behavior is followed immediately by consequences, the likelihood of that behavior being affected are greater than if the consequences are delayed. Example: Rather than waiting until the end of the workshop, time is set aside after each group activity so that members can exchange feedback regarding each other's contributions to the task.
- To acquire behavior, the learner must engage in behavior. Example: Instead of hearing or reading about a new skill or behavior, participants practice it in small groups or by way of a role-play. Following the behaviorist model, the teacher – or some other role model – first explains and demonstrates the skill; learners then practice and receive reinforcing feedback until they achieve the desired competence.[8]

Clear objectives

Robert Mager makes a convincing case for clearly spelled-out objectives. With his landmark book on *criterion-referenced instruction*, he links training content to training outcome: Mager asks teachers to establish measurable criteria that must be met to achieve task-oriented goals. Under the motto that if you don't know where you're going, you won't know when you get there, he shows the value of objectives to course planners, teachers, and learners. What came as a surprise about an otherwise dry subject was Mager's witty writing style and unconventional approach to structuring a book. If you are not familiar with his work, be sure to read at least one of his books. And remember, Mager would say that instruction does not end when the bell rings, but when the student has learned.[9]

Systematic course design

If ever there was a book to bring order into the chaos of course planning, Jerrold Kemp has written it. His system addresses three essential elements of instructional technology: identifying what must be learned (objectives); determining what procedures and resources will work best to reach the desired learning levels (activities and resources); and knowing when the required learning has taken place (evaluation). Step by step, Kemp provides a rationale and detailed description of eight course-planning stages:
- goals and topics
- learner characteristics
- learning objectives
- subject content
- preassessment procedures

Nothing is more dangerous than an idea when it's the only one you have.
– Emile Chartier (1868-1951), French philosopher.

- teaching/learning activities
- support services
- evaluation

The beauty of his approach is its flexibility; we can start anywhere in the process and move backwards and forwards to other steps. Although very structured, Kemp's model suits a wide variety of teaching styles and organization settings. I still recommend it wholeheartedly.[10]

Matching student readiness and teacher style

More recently, I read about an approach to teaching which you and I, intuitively, have practiced for some time. According to Gerald Grow's Self-Directed Learning Model, learners advance through stages of increasing self-direction, and the skilled teacher employs techniques appropriate to each stage. For instance, a "dependent" student at Stage 1, lacking relevant knowledge, skills, and experience, looks for explicit directions of what to do and how to do it and responds well to demonstrations, informal lectures, and supervised practice. At the other end of the spectrum, "self-directed" students at Stage 4 are keen and capable of setting their own goals and standards, with or without help from experts. The appropriate teacher function here is that of consultant and resource person. Problems arise, as happened to me as I began to experiment with learner-centered teaching, when a chosen teaching style does not match learners' readiness.

Grow offers suggestions – but no pat solutions – for classroom applications of his model. He explains how a course, even a single session, can be organized so that students move from dependency, through intermediate stages, to more self-directed learning. If you are interested in this sensible scheme, read his article[11] and, as Grow suggests, become familiar with the Situational Leadership Model he has adapted.[12]

A working theory

Upon reflection, I notice how views that at first were contradictory have become complementary, and now form my *action theory*. It guides me when I teach, helped me to write this book, and evolves as I continue to learn.

The real voyage of discovery consists not in seeking new landscapes but in having new eyes.
– Marcel Proust (1871-1922), French novelist.

2

Planning a session

*If you're not sure where
you're going
you're liable to end up
some place else.*

– Robert Mager

Comments

(1) *This first session includes some quick
introductions and a discussion of course
outline and expectations. The lesson plan
denotes who will do and say what.*

*You'll soon develop your own shorthand.
For instance, if I want to do a warmup
activity during which people team up,
interview each other, and then introduce
their partner to the whole group, the
notation will read: Do interviews. If you
are designing the session for someone
else, instructions have to be more explicit.*

(2) *Estimate the amount of time each component will take. At first try, the time
needed rarely matches the actual time
available and you have to rework your
design. Until I have run through a sequence several times, I make it a habit to
jot down the actual time each segment
takes as the session progresses; this is of
immense help when checking progress
and evaluating the design for future use.*

The Art of Teaching Adults describes ways in which learners and teachers can cooperate to come to terms with course content. However, the countless decisions that precede their encounter in the classroom – the course planning process – are beyond the scope of this book.[1] In your work, you either inherit an existing course design, take the time to devise your own, or simply go in cold. In any case, you'll benefit from having prepared a minute-by-minute schedule, traditionally called a *lesson plan*.

Such a plan, in a nutshell, should outline your objectives, describe your plan of action to reach these objectives, indicate the timing of various segments, list facilities, materials and equipment needed, and provide for ways to measure progress.

A simple lesson plan might look like this.

Time in minutes	Activity (1)
10 (2)	Greet participants and introduce myself: name, qualifications, brief work history, why I like to teach.
10	Hand out the course outlines and briefly explain the course objectives and session plans.
11	Ask participants to form groups of five. Have them go around the group and first introduce themselves by name and affiliation, and then share their reasons for signing up for the course. Each person has two minutes.
6	Ask groups to arrange a flip chart or wall-mounted newsprint. Ask them to take five minutes to record their ideas about the course out-line: additions, deletions, comments. Tell them to just list their ideas, not to edit or prioritize. One person to act as recorder.
9	Help recorders to post their sheets on a wall, side by side. Invite every-one to get out of their seats and gather around. Briefly review the lists and respond. Be clear on which you can accommodate and which you can't. This is important contracting.

A more detailed plan

Min [1]	Obj [2]	Instructor's Activities	Text Page [3]	Learners' Activities [4]	Instructional Devices [5]
10	3.1	Introduce topic of reservations. Ask why they are necessary – and what would happen if there was no such thing. Develop list on board or flipchart. Ask if anyone had experience with making a reservation at a hotel: good or bad experience?		Contribute ideas.	Flip chart, feltpen. Chalkboard, chalk.
5		Describe functions a reservation system must be able to handle, regardless of type of operation, clientele and volume.	p. 81		
10		Explain the routes by which potential guest can reach an operation to make reservation. Explain role of various "agents," the cost and benefits to the hotel.	p. 82		OT #3
20	3.2	Using actual forms for each pair of students, lead them through the filling out of a basic reservation form. Different forms are used, but the basic reason for basic information remains.

Explain terminology and abbreviations used: GTD, 6 pm, VIP, special rate, etc. | p. 86-8 | Working in twos will fill out res. forms from information provided by their partner. [7] | OT #4 |
| | 3.3 | Explain differences in handling individual & group bookings. Who should handle them? | p. 102 | | OT #5 |
| 10 | 3.1 | Explain how/why reservations are charted and how this will differ in approach from one op. to another. The following charting exercise will give students a chance to learn the skills involved. | p. 93 | | OT # 6 OT #7, 7a |
| 60 | | Charting exercise: instructions in package.

Be available for consultation: it is not necessary that everyone finishes it, but that s/he has a good understanding how/why this is done and must be done with precision/care. [6] | | Following instructions and working through the exercise. [6] | HO: *Reservations Charting Exercise* |

From a course on hotel operations

Comments

(1) This column refers to two types of objectives. A learning objective *spells out the educational intent in terms of measurable progress of knowledge, skills, and feelings.*[2] For instance: The learner will be able to distinguish a hawk from an eagle. A process objective, on the other hand, describes desired benefits that are not as easy to quantify. For instance: Learners will work in cooperative teams.

(2) A step-by-step description of content and process. Teaching points are given in some detail to ensure the course content is covered. This segment is heavily weighted towards information-giving by the teacher, but in a short time it incorporates two practice sessions.

(3) Page references to the textbook help teacher and learner.

(4) Planned activities involve participants at different levels of complexity.

(5) Materials and equipment are shown with specific references to prepared overhead transparencies (OT) and handouts (HO).

(6) A lesson plan shows who will do the work. Try to balance activities that are led by the teacher with those in which participants take an active role.

(7) This session includes a practical test to assess learners' comprehension and to flush out questions.

Instructional objectives

"An objective is a description of a performance – behavior, feeling, attitude – you want your learners to be able to exhibit before you consider them competent. Such an objective describes the intended outcome of instruction, rather than the process of instruction itself," writes Robert Mager. *According to his behaviorist view of teaching and learning, everything begins and ends with precise, measurable, and observable descriptions of performance. In one of the most lucid books on educational theory, Mager gives his three main reasons for the importance of objectives.[3]*

1. Objectives are the foundation for course planning.

If clearly defined objectives are absent, there is no sound basis for the selection or designing of instructional materials, content, or methods. If you don't know where you are going, how will you know how to get there?

2. Objectives allow for testing of outcome.

The second major reason for sharply defined objectives has to do with finding out whether the objective has, in fact, been accomplished. If you don't know where you want to go, how will you know that you have arrived?

3. Objectives give clear directions to the learner.

A good objective tells the participant what's going on. With clear objectives, learners are better able to participate in the learning process; they don't have to guess what's expected.

A useful objective communicates your instructional intent by answering three questions.
- *Performance: what should the learner be able to do?*
- *Conditions: under what conditions must the performance occur?*
- *Criterion: how well must it be done?*

The educational viewpoints of "behaviorists" (represented here by Robert Mager) and "humanists" (epitomized by Carl Rogers elsewhere) are considered by some to be polar opposites. However, I have benefited from both in developing a personal theory of adult education.

3 Setting up the room

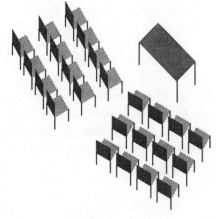

By arranging tables and chairs in a certain way, you set the tone for things to come. A careful setup also communicates your attention to detail and makes that important first impression as participants arrive.

Arrange the room to suit your plan

If you plan to lecture, then rows of seats are fine. If you intend to use small-group activities, ensure the furniture supports your plan. But even if the existing layout is awkward, you can often work around it. If the seats are bolted to the floor, for instance, people can turn around and form a group with the three sitting behind them. If that's your plan, ensure that participants seat themselves in a way that leaves no gaps of empty seats. If the chairs are loosely placed in rows, then groupings can be arranged spontaneously when you give the word.

Take inventory – well in advance

Inspect the facilities, count furniture, notice electrical outlets, examine audio-visual equipment, note windows and doors. Then sketch your desired room setup and discuss it with the person who is in a position to get what you need. But be prepared for surprises: you may arrive and find that things aren't as expected – which brings us to the next point.

Be prepared to arrange at the last moment

In spite of good intentions and advance planning, your room may not be in the condition you expected. You now have to shift furniture yourself and, with a sketch in hand, recruit willing helpers on a moment's notice. Allow extra time for this so that the room is ready when participants arrive. If scheduling does not allow early entry to the room, recruit the first arrivals to help with the setup. There's a warm-up activity for you!

Layout examples

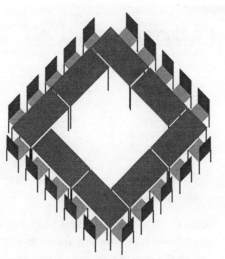

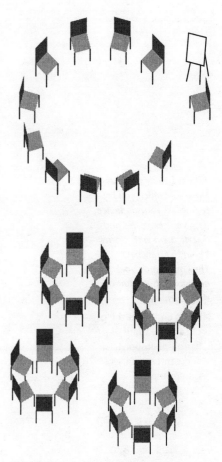

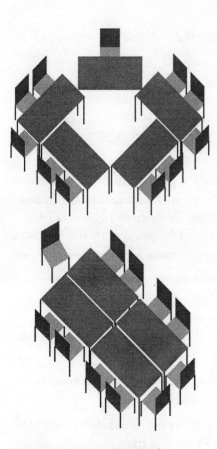

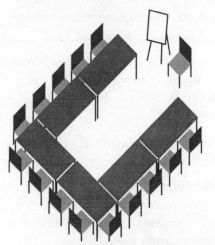

This is a similar setup, but with no designated head table. This layout is ideal when all support materials are in front of the learners. Using a flip chart or overhead projector is possible, but awkward, since one row of participants would have to crane their necks to see.

Here are two setups that simulate a round table, using rectangular tables. This arrangement gives everyone a clear field to see and hear everyone else. Your spot is obviously at the head, next to flip chart or white board.

The popular U-shaped arrangement has several advantages. Participants can see each other when listening and speaking; visual devices are well located; and the facilitator can move into the square to intervene or withdraw to the outside to let the situation flow unhampered. A spare table holds teaching resources and can easily be inserted to create a closed square.

For group activities that focus on discussion, role-playing, problem-solving, and personal sharing, tables are a hindrance. Removing them takes away the "security blanket." By opening up the circle so that everyone is equally exposed, you create a setting that invites participation and interaction.

4

Getting packed

These points are worth considering, especially if you are working in an unfamiliar setting.

☐ Book the room and inspect beforehand. Get to know by name the person who is in charge of room booking and the one who looks after the physical setup. Even when all arrangements are confirmed, you can arrive on a Saturday morning to find the building locked. Who can you phone?

☐ Sketch the room layout to show the desired placement of furniture and audio-visual devices. Discuss it with the person responsible. If possible, confirm in writing. Locate the front of the room away from entrance doors to allow for a traffic flow that will not interfere with the proceedings. To reduce distractions, arrange seating to face a blank wall, rather than doors and windows.

☐ Find and test light switches and electrical outlets. A room that's cool in the morning may heat up considerably when filled with fifty active people. Where are the temperature controls? Can you let in some fresh air?

☐ Check soundproofing. If you'll be working in a room with a portable division, noise may spill over from next door.

☐ Determine whether you can use the walls to post newsprint sheets. Ask to have pictures removed. Assure your hosts that masking tape leaves no marks and that you'll double-sheet and use water-based pens to avoid staining the walls.

☐ Where do the smokers go? Ask your host about house policy. How times change: when I prepared the first edition of this book ten years ago, we still had to figure out seating arrangements for smokers and nonsmokers in the same room.

☐ Check out availability of refreshments. If participants are on their own, determine the distance to vending machines, an in-house cafeteria, or the nearest restaurant. You can reduce confusion and save time by suggesting specific places for people to go and setting realistic break times.

Take teaching seriously. Note how much you try to impress your audience with your expertise and dazzle them with stories "from the trenches." They may enjoy your anecdotes, but what are they learning?

– based on the teachings of Lao Tzu, Chinese hermit-philosopher and contemporary of Confucius.

If refreshments are provided to your group, contact the caterer and coordinate timing and variety. Breaks must include decaffeinated beverages or fruit teas as well as coffee; more and more people look for soft drinks and fruit juices.

☐ Clarify parking arrangements. Determine tow-away zones and parking fees. Find out about special rates for participants of your organization. Let your group know in advance where to park; send maps and clear directions if possible.

☐ Locate access to public telephones and incoming messages. Portable phones and pagers can interrupt the proceedings; ask participants to arrange for no interruptions. During one session with thirty realtors, each carried a pager and almost all had a phone in the briefcase. We agreed not to let the outside interfere with the class work – but at every break there was a mad rush to the phones.

☐ Identify entrance and exits for regular and emergency use. Prepare and post directional signs.

A few words of caution

Always come early and expect the full force of Murphy's Law to descend on you: what can go wrong, will! The possibilities are endless. The person you talk to could go on holidays and leave someone else to set up the room "the way we always do." Frequently you inherit someone else's arrangements (and their mess on the walls and boards). Come prepared for a quick makeover and don't hesitate to ask early arrivals to lend a hand.

To be is to do. – Aristotle
To do is to be. – Socrates
Do be do be do. – Frank Sinatra

Even the best-laid plans are no guarantee. When I was asked to be an after-lunch presenter at a conference, my host had agreed to arrange the furniture to suit brainstorming. I arrived thirty minutes before my allotted time to find that the previous speaker was running late, participants were getting restless, the room was hot and stuffy, sixty instead of forty people were present, chairs stood in rows theater-style with stacks of tables to one side, and an unexpected video crew with bright lights and lapel microphones was adding heat in the room. Some quick thinking, a few laughs, and many helping hands were needed to create a suitable space.

Materials checklist

☐ Flip-chart easel (two are better than one).

☐ Plenty of newsprint paper; have at least one extra pad.

☐ Masking tape.

☐ Felt pens to make notes on flip charts. Use the water-based type (such as Mr. Sketch brand); they smell better and stain less. Test pens and discard old ones.

☐ Transparency pens: water-based ones erase, alcohol-based ones do not. Test pens and discard old ones.

☐ Overhead projector, movable screen, extension cord, spare bulb.

☐ Transparencies: bring blanks as well as prepared ones.

☐ Equipment to play videotapes and films.

☐ Video setup for taping and play-back.

☐ Class registration list.

☐ Handout materials: sorted, stapled, and three-hole-punched.

☐ Name tags and name cards.

☐ Your notes and manuals.

☐ Course-related books and magazines. Place them on a side table for browsing and reference.

☐ Tools: three-hole punch, stapler, staples, pens, pencils, blank writing paper, file cards, clear tape, rubber bands, pliers, (the latter to remove picture hooks and nails, in order to clear a wall to hang flip charts).

☐ Miscellaneous items: band-aid (for nasty paper cuts), headache tablet, breath freshener, comfortable shoes, toiletry kit, personal snacks (fresh fruit, chocolate, or whatever feels good when you work hard).

Come, give us a taste of your quality.

– William Shakespeare,
   Hamlet. Act II, Scene 2.

5

Breaking the ice

When a new group first assembles, participants are usually somewhat awkward and full of questions. Who is here? What's going to happen? Where do I fit in? How safe a place is this? Is this worth my trouble, time, and money? Try to anticipate these concerns by starting off with a warmup activity.

Most adults function best in an atmosphere of respect and support, and even the most self-assured person appreciates some sort of ice-breaking activities. Whichever technique you decide to use, make sure it helps to get people settled in, create a sense of welcome, and establish an atmosphere of collegial cooperation.[1]

What do people want in a first session?

As children, the first day of classes was usually taken up with room assignments, textbook distribution, and timetable discussions; we were pleased to be let out early and have as little instruction as possible. However, adults have different expectations. Good use of time and value for money are important concerns.

Researchers asked adult learners at two Canadian universities about their expectations for a first session.[2] The results suggest that students are more interested in content and the instructor than classmates during the first session. Information about course content, objectives, and expectations rated the highest priority.

But students also wanted to get to know their instructor during that first session. They wanted to know about their instructor's professional and academic background, teaching style, expectations, and availability. They were also interested in each other's backgrounds and reasons for taking a course.

Respondents were split equally between those who wanted early introductions and those who preferred to get acquainted more naturally during refreshment breaks and through group tasks.

Select your activity with care. An exercise that works in one group may bomb in the next. With perfect hindsight, I recall working with a group of health-care managers; my choice of warmup activity fitted them perfectly and they were working together in no time. When I introduced the same activity to an assembly of corrections officers, I sensed trouble right away: my cheerful instructions were met with cold stares and very reluctant responses.

Activity 1: Hello, my name is ...

Names are important to all of us. It is comforting to be addressed by name in a strange environment. The pin-on type is a good beginning to the matching of names and faces. The problem with these tags is that they fall off, are obscured by people's clothing, and usually disappear by the second and third session.

Use double-folded sheets of paper or old file cards as desk-top name cards. Have each person print (in bold letters) the name they want to be called. This should be done on both sides of the card so that it can be seen from different directions. Have brightly colored felt pens on hand. This activity gets you past the awkward Mr./Mrs./Ms./first name/last name quandary. Also, the cards can be brought back for the next session.

Variations

• Ask participants to put their present occupation, affiliation, or anything they consider relevant for identification in small letters in the corners of their name card.

• Ask them to turn the card inside-out and jot down the completion of statements you supply. Use the following examples or improvise your own.

- Right now, I'd rather ...
- I hope this course won't be ...
- I would like to learn ...

While this information is confidential at this stage, you may later wish to ask volunteers to share it with the class. You may also come back to it towards the end of a session or course, when you prompt participants to assess their progress.

Activity 2: Remember me?

This is a further variation of the go-around naming routine. It is best done partway into the course or just before the end of the first session.

• Ask participants to place their chairs in a circle or sit on the table edges. You, too, join the circle.

• Introduce the activity, using your own words along the following lines. "We have been together for a while now and I'd like us to use each other's names whenever possible. Let's play a game you may recall from earlier days. The rules are simple.

"I'll start by telling you my name. The person next to me turns to the person on her right, repeats my name and adds hers, and so we'll go around the circle. When your turn comes you have to try to repeat all the names before yours and then add your own. Don't worry about forgetting a name – you simply ask the person."

• Allow for some reaction to your announcement of this activity, but don't hesitate to remind them that you'll be the last person and will have to remember all the names! This should be good for a few laughs.

How to remember names

- *Pay attention to a new name. If you don't remember it, or hear it clearly the first time, ask the person to repeat it.*

- *Repeat the name yourself. This will improve recall by 30 percent.*

- *Use the name in conversation. Repetition will engrave the name in your long-term memory.*

- *Observe faces. Most of us can remember faces better than names, so really study the face and choose one outstanding detail.*

- *Use the name when saying good-bye. This final reinforcer also ensures that you know the name.*

Activity 3: Press conference

This activity helps to develop team spirit among people who just minutes ago were strangers to each other. It makes useful information available and shows that playfulness is compatible with serious adult education.

Just for the fun of it, have a draw for a book related to the course content. (I buy them at discount sales and spend no more than $5 per class.) We call it Lotto 429 (the class ends at 4:30). Everyone picks a number in the morning and we draw just before closing time.

– Mary Speller is program manager for staff development with the Ministry of Health in Victoria, BC.

1. Explain that group members should assume for a moment that they have been invited to a press conference. This is a chance to query the teacher about the course they're about to begin. Emphasize that the notion of "dumb questions" has been suspended for the duration.

2. Ask participants to form groups of four to five each and pool their questions.

> ### Form groups of four to five
> Decide what questions you want to ask Peter about:
>
> 1. My background
>   My experience
>   My present activities, etc.
>
> 2. The course – Its hours
>   Its contents
>   Tests
>   Practicum
>
> PLEASE ASK ME ANY QUESTIONS THAT YOU FEEL ARE IMPORTANT TO YOU!!

3. Give them six minutes to compile their lists. Suggest that each group take one minute for a quick round of introductions and then use five minutes to work on the list. Ask one member to record the questions in point form.

4. Seat yourself in the "hot seat," ready to be quizzed.

5. When five minutes are up, invite the first representative to pose the first question. From there, proceed from group to group until all questions have been dealt with. Going from group to group and dealing with one question at a time avoids duplication and spreads the questions around the room.

I AM...

- new in my job
- a father of twins
- living in the country
- feeling a bit silly
- a pretty good cook

I AM A RESOURCE
- own my own consulting business
- know about newt-breeding
- have Master's degree in health admin.
- speak Albanian
- collect old maps

Activity 4: Show me

1. Ask each participant to take a blank 8" x 11" sheet of paper and boldly place "I AM ..." as the heading. Then ask everyone to complete the statement in five different ways. (See example at left.)

   Complete a sheet for yourself as well.

2. Once participants have completed their sheets, ask them to hold it in front of them so it can be read by others as they mill about the room.

3. Explain that the rest of the exercise will be done in silence.

4. Ask them to have a look around, mingle, and make nonverbal contact with at least three separate people. Participants should read the lists and gather any additional clues, spending at least thirty seconds with each person they encounter.

5. Some people will need encouragement to move around or reminders to remain silent.

6. After ten minutes of circulating, ask for the sheets to be hung on a wall. Participants may want to have another look during the refreshment break, connecting people and lists.

Variation A

1. Hand everyone a blank piece of paper and a short section of masking tape.

2. Ask participants to put their name in bold letters at the top of the sheet. Next ask them to print five or six words ending with "ing" below their names. These words will serve as their introduction. Examples: reading, cooking, traveling, caring.

   Other word endings may also be used.
   - "able," as in approachable, reasonable, capable, irritable.
   - "ist," as in optimist, pianist, cyclist, specialist.
   - "ful," as in playful, careful, hopeful, delightful.

3. Participants (including you) then hold the sheets up and mill about the room. You can try this with silence for the first two minutes, or you can invite people to meet with two others and share their lists.

Variation B

1. Change the heading to I AM A RESOURCE and invite participants to list their areas of expertise.

2. Stipulate whether or not the list should be confined to the course content or embrace a wider range of know-how and interests. Here's a sample sheet, at left.

Activity 5: Thelma meets Louise

1. Ask students to team up with one of their neighbors. Their task is to spend four minutes interviewing each other and find out at least three things (other than name) about their partner. When the time is up, each participant introduces his or her partner to the large group.

   If people need some help with interview questions, make some suggestions. Why are you taking this course? Where do you come from? How does this course relate to your job/family? What's exciting in your life right now? What do you do when you don't work?

2. After the time is up (gauge it by the amount of talking, but try to keep close to the announced limit), ask people to come back together as a class. You may want to go first, to model the introductions.

3. Ask the person being introduced to stand up so that all can see. Thank everyone for participating.

Activity 6: Listening triads

Ask participants to arrange themselves in groups of three, dispersed about the room for some privacy. Suggest they join with people they know the least.

Give the following instructions.

1. Decide who will be A, B and C in your group.

2. Person A will now tell the others why you are here (or what you expect to learn during this event). Share as much as you are comfortable with. You have two minutes for this.

3. When A's time is up, B and C report back to A what they have heard. A may restate or clarify until he or she is fully understood by B and C. Take no more than two minutes for the feedback phase.

4. Repeat the round until each of you has been in each role.

5. The total time will be twelve minutes. But don't worry about that, I'll call out the times.

The degree to which I can create relationships which facilitate the growth of others as separate persons is a measure of the growth I have achieved in myself.

– Carl Rogers

Activity 7: Expectations revealed

This combines introductions with a sharing of expectations. The survey results provide valuable information for course planning or possible modification.

This activity can be completed in less than fifteen minutes, but will take longer if you expand it into an agenda-building or course-planning session.

There are at least two ways to proceed.

- The quickest and most contained way to gather data is with a questionnaire. Prepare it in advance, listing possible topics, issues, skills, etc.

  Ask participants to check off their most pressing needs, perhaps in order of priority. You can also ask them to add their own items and assign a ranking to them as well. Such a survey can be completed in a few minutes and will provide a quick feel of the communal pulse.

- A more open-ended and less controlled approach requires more time, but may yield unexpected results. Before asking, be clear how much flexibility you have to respond to individual needs.

  The following are samples of questions that will open Pandora's box.

  - I want to learn to ...
  - I learn best when I'm involved in the following activities: ...
  - My expectations of the teacher are ...
  - My expectations of the other participants are ...
  - My contribution to this course could be ...

Once everyone has responded, either in class or by way of a take-home assignment, compile the data or, better, delegate this task to small groups. Assign separate groups to each of the questions and ask them to present their summary to the whole class.

This activity shifts the focus from teacher to learners. You begin the course based on clearly understood expectations. Familiarity with everyone's interests, backgrounds, and needs is invaluable for future session planning.

Variation: Common concerns[3]

This activity takes between five and twenty minutes, depending on the number of participants and the amount of discussion.

Prepare a list of concerns in advance and distribute it at the start of the sessions. The items here are examples only – compose one to suit your

Seek cooperation at every step. You can no more teach without the learner than a merchant can sell without a willing buyer.

– based on the teachings of Lao Tzu.

occasion. As you hand out the list, invite participants to add their own items, or to circle the three items of greatest importance to them.

Which of these ideas has crossed your mind as you prepared for this workshop?
- I won't get my questions answered.
- We'll be doing too much small-group stuff.
- There will be too much lecturing.
- I won't have time to practice the new skills.
- The material will not apply to my situation.
- I'll be expected to make a presentation.
- Discussions will take up too much time.
- Breaks will go on for too long.
- Our backgrounds will be too diverse.
- I won't learn anything new.

Participants first work alone, marking their most important items. Then ask them to discuss the items with others. Depending on the group size, this can be done by the whole group, in pairs, or small groups of three to five. Write up the most-often-raised issues on a flip chart, respond to the concerns, and leave the list up as a reminder for all.

Use this activity only if you are prepared to discuss and even change some aspects of the course design. Inevitably, there will have to be some give and take between you and the participants. The beauty of this activity is that it starts a cooperative process that can carry on throughout the course.

Activity 8: Learning needs

Use this to establish the expectations of your group. But be fully prepared to respond and, if necessary, make changes to your instructional plans.

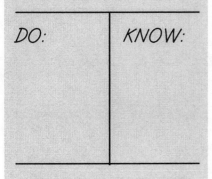

By Friday I want to be able to:

DO: | KNOW:

HAVE EXPERIENCED:

1. To begin, post the chart illustrated at left. If you have ten or fewer participants, one sheet will suffice: everyone can take turns recording ideas on it. Ask that they use key words and print boldly with colored felt pens. If your numbers are larger, ask small groups of five or six to work together.

2. Interrupt the recording when a good number of ideas has been recorded. If working in groups, post the sheets where everyone can see them.

3. Invite participants to form a semicircle and look over the sheets. Let the discussion run for a few minutes so that everyone has a chance to read all lists.

4. Respond to the posted expectations. Do they match what you have planned? Which can you accommodate and which lie outside the course parameters? Note all similarities between group lists and your own design. If possible, offer suggestions for individuals whose expectations cannot be met.

This activity will demonstrate your interest in everyone's needs and your approach to conflict.

Activity 9: Agenda-building

If your course design is open to modifications, make the building of a joint agenda a warmup activity.

1. Present a summary of your course goals. Make it clear that they are here to guide the participants, not dictate to them.

2. Help the group to express its goals and to build an agenda for the next session(s).[4] Guided by consensus, the group might decide on content, assign responsibilities, and manage its own time.[5] Here's an example of a group agenda.

AGENDA

CONTENT	WHO	PROCESS	TIME
What we've done since last week	Mary	Starting up	15'
Goals and agenda	Reg	Discussion	10'
Planning models	Reg	Lecturette	20'
Needs assessment	George	Group exercise	60'
Group critique	All	Round-the-room	12'
Goals for next session	Reg	Handout	3'

This chart was suggested by Reg Herman

Topics are listed down the left-hand column, with names of the person responsible. The right-hand columns show the techniques to be used and an approximation of the time available for each topic.

Activity 10: Unfinished statements

This one takes only ten minutes and is especially suitable for large assemblies.

1. Greet participants and tell them the activity will take about ten minutes.

2. Ask them to listen to an unfinished statement and think of ways to complete it. For example: the one thing I like about teaching ...; the main reason I'm here ...; the thing that frustrates me most about my current job .... (Choose a sentence that suits your group.)

3. Write the sentence stem on the board or overhead projector.

4. Ask participants to get up and make contact with one person at a time. Ask them to share their sentence completion and, if appropriate, seek elaboration. Instruct participants to move around the room and take no more than sixty seconds for each encounter.

5. Let the activity continue for five to ten minutes, enough time for everyone to meet at least five different people.

6. Monitor the process by moving around the room, listening inconspicuously to the encounters. If people wander off the topic, remind them to stick to the exchange of statements. If necessary, adjust the timing for each meeting.

7. Conclude the activity by asking participants to return to their seats. As an optional add-on, ask for volunteers to share their reactions to what they have just heard.

Activity 11: Predicting success

This has become a favorite opening with task-oriented groups; it subtly informs participants of their responsibility for the session's outcome.

1. Post the heading: What has to happen for this course (or session) to be a success?

2. Ask participants to call out descriptions of what they'd consider evidence of success. The chart on the next page shows some examples, recorded in such a way as to distinguish content from process issues. If the numbers warrant it, ask people to form groups of five to six members and have each group complete a sheet. Five minutes are probably enough.

WHAT HAS TO HAPPEN
FOR THIS COURSE TO BE A SUCCESS?

- Clear learning goals
- Instructor shares her expertise
- We tap participants' expertise
- Regular progress checks
- Up-to-date research data
- Relevant to back-home needs

- Everyone gets involved
- We don't waste time
- Students have a say on agenda
- Short, focused lectures
- Team projects
-

3. Post the sheets side-by-side and lead a brief discussion of the entries. Explore how these expectations relate to the course agenda.

4. Throughout the course, refer to the success statements to keep the group focused on their desired outcome.

CLASSIC CONCEPT

The aging learner

With more and more older persons participating in adult education activities, the effects of physiological aging are a concern for planners and teachers. Patricia Cross has summarized research about the probable effect of certain physical changes on learning.[6]

- Reaction time

"As people grow older, they slow down. Speed of learning involves reaction time to perceive a stimulus, transmission time to transmit the message to the brain, and response time to carry out the action. On the average, older learn-ers perceive more slowly, think more slowly, and act more slowly than younger people. In general, the time required for learning new things increases with age."

- Vision

"As eyes age, there is a loss of elasticity and transparency, pupils become smaller and react more feebly, and there is an increasing incidence of cataracts and defective color vision. While almost everyone recognizes the need for bifocals as a sign of aging, not everyone is aware of the need for increased illumination. A fifty-year old is likely to need 50 percent more light than a twenty-year old."

- Hearing

"Aging brings problems with pitch, volume, and rate of response. Rapid speech, for example, can result in loss of intelligibility of up to 45 percent of older people. Women seem to lose acuity for lower pitch, while men lose it for high pitch, making older women able to communicate more readily with women while older men can hear men's voices better."

6

Contracting for learning

A contract is a written agreement specifying mutual expectations between two or more persons. The term "contract" underscores that such an accord is legitimate, fair, and possible.

Learning contracts can be used for a wide variety of subjects and course formats. They acknowledge that adult groups are not homogenous: participants arrive from widely differing backgrounds and are motivated by assorted needs. Contracts can provide choices to people who have separate aspirations and abilities.

If you are trying a contract for the first time, start with one that opens just a few components to negotiation. This way you and the participants can enter your new relationship with little anxiety. Here are some items that can easily be individualized.

- individual learning goals

- steps to be completed to reach the goals

- specified reading and out-of-class preparation

- nature of class participation

- method of evaluation or grading

- attendance requirements

- topic and format of individual projects

Learners and instructor each keep a signed and dated copy. At evaluation times, it forms the basis for assessment and possible changes. A learning contract is an important step towards establishing a community of learners. It reinforces participants' responsibility for their own learning. It also specifies the teacher's functions and responsibilities.

In addition to their use in short-term courses and workshops, contracts offer interesting possibilities in career and management development programs. In such circumstances, a learner might make an agreement with a teacher, mentor, supervisor, or even a support group. Such contracts could pertain to on-the-job training programs, independent learning projects, or any professional development sequence.

Case study:
the contracting process

This contract lets the students decide the end-of-course evaluation and potential grade. It was used in a course called *Effective Interpersonal Relations*, where some came for professional development, others for university transfer, still others for personal growth alone. While course content and process were controlled by the faculty – and were not negotiable – students selected the workload associated with each potential grade. According to Malcolm Knowles, the contracting process should include nine steps.[1]

1. The learner selects a realistic goal for the undertaking and then breaks it into achievable subgoals.

2. A competency model is developed, consisting of the knowledge, attitudes, and skills required to meet each subgoal.

3. Present levels of competency are first documented, then contrasted with desired levels.

4. Based on the gaps between present and desired competencies, learning needs are identified.

5. Existing and potential learning resources are identified and matched to learning needs.

6. A practical schedule for completion is established.

7. Criteria and acceptable evidence for evaluation are specified.

8. A support network and reward structure is identified and agreed upon.

9. The contract is carried out and evaluated.

Sample learning contract

1. What you can expect to gain from the course
- knowledge of communication and helping skills
- ability to attend, observe, listen, and respond more accurately
- ability to express yourself more clearly and constructively
- increased awareness of your self, feelings, thoughts

2. What you can expect from the instructor
- to model the skills and qualities being taught so you can see how they work
- to lecture clearly so the skills and the theory can be understood
- to train you (in small groups) in the use of the skills
- to be available for consultation about personal concerns related to the course outside class (not long-term counseling)

3. What the course expects of you
- to attend all forty-five hours of the course; anyone absent for nine hours or more may be asked to take the course over
- to read assigned readings outside of class and complete the pre-discussion questions
- to participate in small groups and share some personal, but not deep, issues
- to practice skills outside of class

4. Grading criteria and procedures
If you do not want a grade
- you can choose to audit. As an audit student you pay fees, and attend classes, and participate fully, but are not required to submit a videotape for evaluation.

You can expect a "pass"
- if you demonstrate your skills in class

at the "C" level (described below); you are not required to do a videotape for final evaluation.

You can expect to receive an "A" if you are able to
- attend, observe, listen, and respond specifically (as described in the manual)
- help others personalize a problem (as described in the manual)
- demonstrate an overall understanding of the helping model presented in this course in a written essay exam
- help someone personalize a problem on the video final

You can expect to receive a "B" if you are able to
- attend, observe, listen, respond effectively (as described in the manual)
- demonstrate an overall understanding of the helping model presented in this course in a written essay exam (final)
- help someone personalize a problem on the video final

You can expect to receive a "C" if you are able to
- attend, observe and listen accurately and respond specifically to others in the class
- demonstrate an overall understanding of the helping model presented in this course in a written exam (final)

Learner-centered teaching

Psychologist Carl Rogers conceptualized "client-centered therapy" and later developed a parallel theory about adult education. Based on his observations that "therapy is a learning process," he puts forth some basic hypotheses of "student-centered teaching."[2]

- We cannot teach anyone directly; we can only facilitate a person's learning.

- A person learns significantly only those things which are perceived as applicable in the maintenance or enhancement of the structure of self.

- If an experience involves a change in the organization of the self, learners are likely to resist it. A person's boundaries tend to become rigid when threatened, relaxed when free from threat.

- Any experience perceived as inconsistent with the self can only be assimilated if the current organization of self is relaxed and expanded to include it.

- The educational situation that most effectively promotes significant learning is one in which threat to the self of the learner is reduced to a minimum.

Rogers suggests we shift the spotlight from teacher to individual learners. Throughout the entire course design, he calls on us to question the relevance of every course requirement, entrance exam, assignment, project, classroom activity, lecture topic, and evaluation procedure.

Rogers proposes we involve learners in the important aspects of course design and management. He advocates delineation of accountability so that teacher and learner become jointly responsible for a positive outcome.

Rogers also directs us to the creation of an environment perceived as safe and supportive by all participants – a climate that encourages risk-taking, questioning the old, and trying out the new. Directions and feedback, to be most helpful, must be given with caring attention to individual needs.

7

Working in groups

Buzz groups are the workhorse of interactive teaching. "Buzz" refers to the sound emitted by groups of adults concentrating on a task. Occasionally the label "Phillips 66" is used, acknowledging the colleague who first wrote about "small groups of six people working together for six minutes."

Buzz groups are spontaneously formed teams with a task to be accomplished in a short time. Their assignments may be about idea-generating, brainstorming, information-sharing, question-gathering, list-making, or problem-solving.

Typically, one person acts as recorder, noting and summarizing the group's output, and reporting to the larger group afterwards. The teacher stays out of the way, but monitors the progress of the groups and offers procedural guidance and content suggestions as needed.

Buzz groups are best used to ...
- stimulate individual input
- break the ice at the outset
- warm up the class to a new topic
- measure previous knowledge and experience
- generate lists of questions
- gather opinions and identify preconceived ideas
- rank-order items to create an agenda
- obtain feedback on virtually any topic
- tackle a wide range of problems
- elicit ideas on classroom procedures
- ensure individual "air time," regardless of class size and time restraints

Group size

The size of a basic buzz group is best kept between three and six members. If groups are larger, members tend to seek smaller, less confusing subgroups. But even your largest class can be divided into several small groups; it's quite possible, for instance, to divide 120 people into 20 small groups and spread them across a meeting room.

Time required

Allow four to six minutes for the buzz, as well as time for your initial instructions, the grouping process, and subsequent reporting. As participants become better acquainted with this technique, they also become more efficient and very little time is wasted.

Materials needed

Depending on the reporting procedure (see step 9 below), each group may need newsprint, felt pens, and masking tape.

Room setup

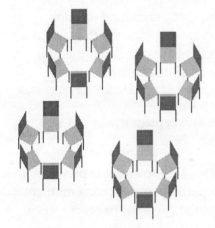

If chairs are movable, ask learners to shift so they can face each other. If seats are fixed to the floor (in an auditorium), two to three people turn to those seated behind them to form buzz groups.

How to proceed

1. Explain the procedure.

Most adults are familiar with teacher-centered schooling, and they appreciate a few words of explanation whenever you ask them to become active participants. Be quite explicit in your introduction: "Now that I have laid out my plan for the day, I'd like to hear what you think. Since we are quite a large group it would take too long for everyone to be heard in turn, so let's do it in small groups. You'll be sitting with four or five other members for a few minutes to respond to a question I shall post. One of you will be the recorder and be asked to report to the large group on what you've each had to say. This way everybody will be heard, first in the small group, then by way of the recorder. How does that sound? Do you have any questions before we proceed?"

2. Form buzz groups.

Be honest. If someone asks a question you can't answer, say so. Maybe another group member knows. Often the one who asked already has part of the answer inside. Offer to find out or ask for volunteers to investigate and report back.

Have participants turn to others sitting nearby and form groups of four to six. Give specific directions, such as "Turn to the people sitting near you," or "Get together with someone you know least," or "This time, I'd like you to team up with people who work in settings similar to yours." Initially, this grouping will take a bit of time, but don't let that deter you. The benefits of learner-involvement compensate for the time spent; adults become quite adept at choosing groups and on subsequent occasions groups are formed with little delay.

3. Describe the task.

The task must be something that can be accomplished in five or six minutes. If it is larger, divide it up and deal with each piece in turn. If, by design or accident, a task is larger than the time available, you'll have to think of ways to deal with the loose ends. With all the commotion in the room, it is best to write the task on the board, flip chart, or overhead. Leave it in plain view throughout the discussion; groups frequently refer to it to stay on track. Clear language is important, as in the example at left.

4. Specify a time limit.
Four to six minutes are typical time spans for small tasks. On average, each group member has a minute of air time. Anything less leads to crowding; anything longer invites tuning-out, wandering off topic, and social chit-chat. Time restraints help groups focus on the task. You must gauge this element carefully and expand and contract the time allowance to suit the task and the maturity of the participants.

5. Ask for recorders.
Suggest that each group select a recorder and explain the recorder's job.

6. Recommend a process.
This applies mainly to inexperienced groups. Following the previous example of agenda-building groups, ask participants to take a moment to introduce themselves, then go around the circle so that each person can state one item to be added to the agenda. Those who are satisfied with the existing agenda should say so. Then it's the next person's turn, until every member has had equal air time. If a group has spare time, go around again to catch additional ideas. Ask groups to assist their recorder in registering each contribution.

You may ask that recorders add contributors' names in brackets next to each item for future reference. To sharpen the focus on the task, you can further stipulate a specific number of items to be generated.

7. Monitor progress.
Circulate from group to group to unobtrusively listen in as they go about their work. This is not a time to relax: it is vital that you are alert to monitor each group's progress, ready to make brief interventions to steer groups and recorders towards the accomplishment of their task. But take care not to interfere too much, since a group quickly develops its own personality.

8. Act as timekeeper.
Time does fly when buzz groups get together. By announcing "halfway through" or "two minutes remaining" you help groups with their task and remind everyone of their share of air time. Should you sense that more time would be of benefit, feel free to announce a schedule change. Example: "You are all working so hard – please take an extra three minutes to complete the list. I remind each group member to

ensure that your views have been accurately recorded"; "If your group is already finished, please look over your list once more, and make any additions you think are important."

9. Invite the recorders to report.
If you are working with just a handful of groups, the simplest procedure is to ask one recorder after another to stand up and report. Alternatively, ask the recorders to post the summary sheets of their group's findings on a blank wall.

10. Process the information.
If you want people's input, you need to acknowledge their contributions and then act on them. In the agenda-building example we have used here, the negotiations could now center on incorporating the learners' agendas with that of the teacher.

Variations

Multiple uses for buzz groups

- Buzz groups can be used as a warmup with new groups. Ask group members to first introduce themselves and then share one or two expectations for the course. This serves as a starting point for a discussion on what is desirable and possible to accomplish. Adults appreciate being involved from the outset and in having a say in how time is spent.

- Use buzz groups prior to a lecture. Buzz groups can tell you what's already known about the topic, what people expect to learn, and which aspects are of particular interest.

- Intersperse a lecture with buzz groups to foster comprehension and bring out questions.

- Conclude a lecture by asking groups to integrate new information with previous learning. They can be asked to identify remaining problem areas or explore practical applications of theoretical material.

- Preceding or following a complex course component, ask buzz groups to collect questions and issues that need clarification.

- Buzz groups are an ideal vehicle for various assessments. In a supportive climate, people will make constructive comments on course content and instructor performance, as long as there is a safe way to do this. Working in small groups, free-style or with an evaluation form, participants can provide valuable information – without having to face the teacher directly. Recorders, speaking on behalf of others, are more at ease in reporting sensitive information.

[The teacher] only helps all creatures to find their own nature, but does not venture to lead them by the nose.

– Lao Tzu, *Tao Teh Ching*. Tao, or the Way, emphasizes simplicity, naturalness, and spontaneity in all essentials of life.

Reporting techniques

- Not all groups need to report individually, only those who have something new to contribute. This reduces repetition and encourages enthusiastic participation the next time you ask the class to work in groups.

- If the task involves list-making, ask groups to collect their ideas first, and then rank the items in some order – by importance or urgency, for example. During subsequent reporting and action-planning, rankings simplify the processing.

- Have recorders report only one point per turn. This avoids situations where the first group reports the bulk of the information, preventing others from contributing.

- Ask various recorders to post their reports side-by-side on a wall. Have recorders briefly describe their lists, elaborate as necessary, and answer questions from the audience. It'll be hard work for them. Ask them to skip items that have already been mentioned. Throughout, you act as process consultant – let the group do the work.

- Reverse the flow of information: instead of taking it to the group at large, have participants circulate from posting to posting. Ask that one member stay behind and act as interpreter. After participants have had time to check out other lists, they return to their own.

There they briefly report what they have learned and then make any changes and additions to their own work. Conclude this round by asking for verbal reports on significant learnings.[1]

Group size

Asking participants to arrange themselves into small groups is easily said, but the novice participant may be hesitant or uncertain and hold back. However, if handled with some sensitivity, small-group activities yield valuable benefits in the form of increased participation and commitment.

Small-group activities offer several advantages. While lectures and other instructor-centered activities invite learner passivity, small-group tasks require and encourage active engagement of all participants. In small groups people have less chance to hide or get lost.

Researchers have found that participants tend to speak more freely in small groups than in large ones; that in large groups people feel little or no personal responsibility for the success of the course; and that participating in small-group tasks increases individual commitment dramatically.

- **Two people (diads)**
  This size of group works only with people who know and trust each other. Members tend to feel intensely responsible to one another, avoid expressing disagreement or antagonism, and feel obliged to adjust to the other's preferences and style of behavior. If one member withdraws, the group becomes ineffective.

- **Three people (triads)**
  This is the minimum-sized group where a coalition can form; the group can still function (as a diad) if one member withdraws or does not cooperate. Creative and innovative ideas are more likely to develop here than in a group of two.

- **Two to five people (small groups)**
  From all indications this is the ideal size for task-oriented groups.

- **Six to ten people (medium-sized groups)**
  Once a group exceeds five members, there is a tendency for subgroups to form and go off on tangents. Participants may then complain of a lack of coordination, insufficient opportunity to have a say, and poor use of time. Accomplishments tend to be of poorer quality. Face-to-face interactions and the care and consideration that are associated with them become difficult if there are more than eight people. Personal statements are not made, and people tend to experience less personal satisfaction and involvement with the group's activities.

Small-group dynamics

M. E. Shaw[2], after searching the literature on small group behavior, reported the following.

- **Seating arrangements**
  People followed the person across from them in speaking more often than those in any other position.

- **Table shapes**
  Interesting behavior was observed with rectangular tables. Those sitting at the two ends of the table participated more than others in the group.

- **Eye contact**
  The possibility of having eye contact with group members tends to increase interaction, regardless of relative seating distance. Women communicate with eye contact more frequently than men.

- **Leadership**
  The probability that a leader will emerge increases with increasing group size. The individual with special skills relating to the group task is usually more active in the group, makes more contributions towards the task, and has more influence on group decisions. The anxious group member inhibits group functioning, and (you guessed it) the well-adjusted member contributes to the group's functioning.

- **Age**
  Social participation increases with increasing chronological age. Group leaders tend to be older than other group members; there is a slight tendency for physically superior individuals to become leaders.

8

Delivering lively lectures

Build on your strengths and stick to techniques that are comfortable. From there experiment with unfamiliar ones: be cautious, but whole-hearted. You might tell the class: "I'd like to try something different that I've never tried before. Are you game to see how it'll work for us?" Success becomes a shared responsibility.

Why does lecturing have such a poor reputation? You probably have your own recollection of past events: boring, inefficient, a waste of time. Just a few are remembered favorably: they captured our imagination, stimulated our thinking, and propelled us to explore the topic on our own. The content of others, less helpful and downright annoying, we have long forgotten, although the memory lingers. Yet, in spite of its controversial reputation, the lecture remains the mainstay of educational practice.

Few instructors seem to be comfortable with lecturing, and even fewer adult participants look forward to it; it is simply endured as part of classroom learning. Yet we also know that a good presentation can bring even the most complicated or dry subject to life and turn passive listeners into active participants. So, what do we need to understand about this technique, in order to turn dreaded lectures into delightful discourses?

Best use of the lecture

Institutional traditions often suggest that you use the lecture as the primary teaching technique. Before you automatically succumb to these expectations, be sure that it's the best method for the task. The lecture's best uses are in the following situations.

- To establish the general outlines of your subject matter. Use the lecture to provide an overview of the topic.

- To arouse interest in a topic. Use it to share your general enthusiasm for the subject. Make important connections between the students' needs, your own interests, and the topic. Show how the participants might benefit from a further exploration of the material.

- To demonstrate how to approach a field of study and make sense of much data. By the structure of your lecture and the way you present your material, you show participants how to deal with a vast body of information.

- To provide information. If you are clear on the learning needs of your audience and present information with clarity and enthusiasm, the lecture may be the most efficient method.

- To mix passive and active techniques. Listening to someone speak to a large group for an extended period of time is essentially a passive activity. The average attention span in such a setting has been estimated at somewhere between twelve and twenty minutes.[1] Even if your schedule calls for a one-hour lecture, you are still free to cut it into short segments peppered with some of the involvement techniques mentioned in this book.

When not to lecture

The lecture is of limited value if students are expected to master complex, abstract, or very detailed material. The lecture also has limitations when dealing with matters pertaining to participants' feelings and attitudes. It can be used to describe and argue such matters theoretically and give the lecturer a chance to share personal experiences, but it does not allow for individual interaction.

What students expect from us

When asked for their opinions on lecturers,[2] adult learners tell us that they look for someone who can ...

- demonstrate knowledge of the topic
- follow a well-organized presentation
- capture and hold attention
- use relevant examples and applications
- show genuine enthusiasm
- involve the audience, directly or indirectly
- respond to questions with respect
- use humor

The AIDA format makes it easy to address most of these points.[3] The acronym stands for "attention," "interest," "desire," and "action."

To gain the group's *attention*, allow a few minutes at the outset of the lecture for people to settle in. Begin right away to establish your competence as speaker as well as content specialist. Restate the topic of the lecture and outline your plan for the amount of time you have allotted. If applicable, spell out learning objectives and make reference to previous materials and events. A story, an anecdote, a cartoon, or a startling statistic can all help to draw attention to you and your presentation.

Teachers as actors

To distinguish good from poor, Californian researchers arranged for regular teachers as well as briefed actors to give a series of college lectures. Students were unaware of the experiment, and when end-of-term results were compared, those taught by the actors did better than those with regular teachers. Another study, at Tel Aviv University, showed that in courses taught by professors who had been coached to use humor, students fared 15 percent better on exams than their colleagues in laugh-free classrooms.

Next, get the group *interested* in what you have to say, by showing the relevance of your presentation to their situation. Offer a preview and touch on highlights of things to come. Address unspoken questions about content and procedures. Why is this important? What are the qualifications of the lecturer? What can I expect to learn? What is expected of me? Will we be able to ask questions? What else will we do during this session? Will there be a break? Should I take notes?

The *desire* part of AIDA alludes to your personal commitment to the topic and how you present it. This is reflected in the thoroughness of your preparation, the use of visuals, relevant examples, and your enthusiasm. The latter is conveyed especially by your alert posture, sweeping eye contact, timing, and use of voice. Ignite participants' desire by making repeated connections between your material and their knowledge and experience.

Finally, *action* describes the way you act before the group. Be conscious of the standards you set by being prompt, prepared, organized, attentive, respectful, sensitive, and honest. You can encourage learners to take an active role in several ways.[4]

- Interrupt the lecture to ask for examples of the concepts you have presented or answer spot quiz questions.
- Ask them to briefly turn to their neighbors to compare notes, pool questions, solve puzzles, and teach each other.
- Assign specific listening tasks to individuals or small groups. Following a lecture segment, teams gather to share concerns, generate questions, and work on applications.
- Lecture for a while, then stop. Pose a case study and invite small groups to analyze it in the context of the material you have just presented.

Time required

Experience suggests that no lecture should last longer than thirty minutes. In other words, try to limit your straight lecturing to between twenty and thirty minutes. At that point utilize any technique that requires participants to switch from passive to active behavior, from listening to doing. There is no reason why you could not have a one- or even two-hour lecture, as long as you mix up the techniques and keep your participants involved.

Variation

A *lecturette* is a short lecture lasting not more than ten minutes. It is a handy way to break a complex topic into several small ones, interspersing other learning activities to aid in understanding and comprehension. If this variation appeals to you, but you aren't sure that you can stick to the ten-minute limitation, try something that's worked for me. Set a kitchen timer, place it in full view of the group, and explain what you are attempting. By letting your group in on the experiment, you not only get their attention, but also involve them in the mechanics of teaching.

Materials needed

None for the lecture, unless you think visual aids would help you make the point better.

Room setup

Each participant should have a full view of the lecturer. You can enhance this by moving around, either on the designated platform or throughout the room.

Nine ways to renovate your lectures

---

1. Set limits.
Limit the scope of the lecture: six major points are enough for half an hour.

2. Outline your plan.
Specify what you plan to cover, how long it will take, and how you plan to proceed. This helps participants anticipate events, prepare for change in technique, and allot their energy accordingly.

3. Provide summaries.
At the beginning, the end, and occasionally in the middle, pause to give listeners a chance to catch up and summarize for themselves.

4. Use visual supports.
Use flip charts, overheads, skits, models, demonstrations, and critical incidents to grab learners' attention and support your points.

5. Utilize handouts.
Save time and disruptions when handing out materials. Instead of one sheet at a time, give it all out at once, with pages numbered or color-coded. Or situate materials in strategic spots and, on your request, ask volunteers to distribute to their group or row of seats.

6. Pace yourself.
Adjust your rate of speaking and choose your vocabulary to fit the experience level of your group. Build in checks to see if everybody understands the points you are making. Do this by asking questions, posing hypothetical cases, or assigning small-group tasks.

7. Keep 'em interested.
Mix activities so that students can be alternately passive (sit, hear, see) and active (problem-solve, write, construct, discuss, move, walk, speak, operate equipment).

8. Sequence deliberately.
Structure material in a logical way: go from the general to the specific, the simple to the complex, the old to the unfamiliar. And every so often – just to keep everyone from becoming stale – reverse this order.

9. Attend to questions.
Clearly state how and when questions will be dealt with. Do you want to hear questions any time something is unclear or do you want them held until you ask for them? You might suggest that participants jot down their questions and raise them at a designated time. But if you say you'll handle questions, do so and allow sufficient time.

Spirited question-and-answer sessions

When addressing large groups, the opportunities for individual attention are limited ... until you get to questions. Here are some tips used by seasoned speakers.[5]

- Take questions from all parts of the room. Don't restrict yourself to people sitting in the front row. Don't let special interest groups monopolize you.

- Listen carefully to each question. Don't frown or smile as you listen – reserve your response until you answer.

- Mind your body language. Avoid motions that might convey uncertainty or lack of interest. Try not to show your approval or disapproval of the questioner's viewpoint or manner of asking.

- Look at each questioner until you understand the question, then direct your answer to the whole audience. This keeps you from getting stuck in an exchange with just one person and invites others to join in.

- Treat each questioner as equal. Avoid the "Good question!" compliment; however sincere, it suggests that you are evaluating the quality of the question and some are better than others. Show respect and curiosity for each question. You did ask for them!

- Repeat questions in full or at least paraphrase them. This ensures that you have understood, gives others a chance to fully hear it, and even gives you a moment to collect your thoughts.

- Respond simply and directly. Use the time to clarify and reinforce points you made during the lecture, not to make impromptu speeches or major additions. If the questions go too far off the topic, state limitations to refocus the group. If questions are slow in coming, be prepared to prime the pump – or move on to other activities.

- Encourage questions right up to the time limit, but avoid saying, "We have time for one more question." If it turns out to be a difficult one or one that raises important further points, you'd end on a "down" tone. Instead, choose a question and answer that makes a good ending and simply end there.

- Use buzz groups. If you are working with a large audience and you expect more questions than time permits, consider asking people to turn to their neighbors and form groups of three to four. Ask them to quickly pool their questions on a piece of paper and assign a priority rating to the list. One person acts as spokesperson for each group, raising one question at a time. Group by group, you ask for their next-most-important question. Those already posed by others are deleted from the list as you proceed.

Just how funny are you?

Used at the right moment and without giving offence, humor certainly lightens up the day. I don't tell jokes, but rely on situational humor and anecdotes to connect with my audience. Humor research (yes!) is inconclusive on the beneficial effects of humor on learning and retention, but "appropriate self-disparaging humor" can reduce students' anxiety by letting them know that the teacher is human and fallible.[6]

Communications professor Charles Gruner suggests that humor may increase your "character" rating, but have little impact on the "authoritativeness" of what you say. If you think you have a good joke or anecdote, he offers this test. Unless you can say "yes" to every question, cut it out![7]

- *Will it fit the subject and mood of my lecture?*

- *Will every person feel comfortable with it?*

- *Is it fresh, short, and uncomplicated?*

- *Can I deliver it with confidence and perfect timing?*

How to get everyone's attention

- *Change your position. Move around, speak from the back of the room, the front, the left or the right of the room. I have been known to stand on top of a table to make a point.*

- *Use gestures. Hand, head, and body movements can serve as supporters (and distracters) for verbal output.*

- *Focus attention. Say something like, "I was shocked to read that ...," or, "Look at this peculiar graph ...."*

- *Vary the style of interaction. Use questions, student-student interactions, buzz groups, demonstrations, problem-solving, tasks, discussions.*

- *Let silence work for you. Use it to encourage reflection, question formulation, and concentration.*

- *Change tempo. With voice tone, volume, and speed, fluctuate between loud and mellow, fast and slow, happy and sad, matter-of-fact and personal, fluent and hesitant.*

Please take notes

"Fill in the blanks" is a useful way to assist learners in note-taking and ensure that they focus on your main points. As you make your important points, participants can fill in the blanks on the handout you have prepared. They learn by seeing and hearing as you speak, but also by repeating in writing.

Fill in the blanks

Topic: Managing Conflict

Principles:

    1. Conflict is _____.

    2. Conflict can be desirable when it is _____.

    3. Uncontrolled conflict is

    _____.

Controlled Conflict:

    1. Deal with conflict _____.

    2. Identify the _____ problem.

    3. Handle _____.

    4. Consider the _____ traits involved.

    5. Ask for _____ and proposed solutions.

    6. Avoid _____, use logic.

    7. Think it _____.

    8. Schedule a _____ session.

Contributed by Susan Reuthe.

9

Asking beautiful questions

John Dewey has said that the aim of education must be "the formation of careful, alert, and thorough habits of thinking." The best questions, those that are truly instructive, are formulated with care and posed with sensitivity. In this section you'll find some essential dos and don'ts, along with proven techniques to assist you in developing your questioning skills.

The best question has as its primary goal the promotion of thinking. As the ancient proverb states:

> I hear, I forget.
> I see, I remember.
> I do, I understand.
> I think, I learn.

In one study, researchers found that two-thirds of the questions asked in a typical classroom required only recitation of a memorized text as a satisfactory answer. A subsequent investigation concluded that the overwhelming proportion of questions asked by college professors were on the memory level. The first study was conducted in 1912 and the second, more than seventy years later.[1] Apparently little has changed. Through the ages, most teachers have asked rote questions designed to get the "right" answer, to "cover the text," and "prepare students for exams."

When we become teachers ourselves, we often draw on our own educational experiences for guidance. And since most of our teachers (in schools and on the job) rewarded the "right answer" above all else, trainers and adult educators unconsciously continue that tradition. Can we break the mold? Yes, if we have the courage and the stamina. The tools have been around for at least forty years. In 1956 Benjamin Bloom and his associates published a six-level model for use with achievement tests and classroom questions.[2] They proposed a taxonomy with six cognitive (thinking) operations arranged in a hierarchy, each level subsuming those preceding it. Here they are, in ascending order. Use them to vary the complexity of your questions.

Level 1: Knowledge – the ability to remember material previously learned.

Level 2: Comprehension – the ability to grasp the meaning of material.

Level 3: Application – the ability to use learned material in new, concrete situations.

Level 4: Analysis – the ability to break down material into its components so that its organizational structure can be understood.

Level 5: Synthesis – the ability to put parts together to form a new whole.

Level 6: Evaluation – the ability to judge the value of material for a given purpose.

Lecturing usually covers the material faster than the more ponderous asking of questions. But questioning shifts the focus from teacher to learners; instead of monopolizing discussions, the teacher becomes a facilitator and participants gradually increase responsibility for their own learning.

One colleague, after experimenting with higher-order questioning, reported that his learners "pay attention; they listen to each other and give answers that show that they are thinking about what they are going to say. I find that the quality of their questioning has also improved; they seem to have a better understanding of the concepts and are showing improvements in tests and written work."[3]

Questions about questions ... with answers by Dr. Scott Parry[4]

The way you ask a question has a lot to do with the answer you get. For a group to work together effectively, everyone's ideas must be heard. Effective questioning is a necessary skill for facilitating a training seminar. To get everyone involved and learning, you have to know what to ask, how, and of whom. You have to know how to give every learner a chance to come up with her or his own solutions.

Questions are one of your most valuable tools – for making points, for assessing understanding, for arousing interest, and for testing understanding. Most trainers would agree. Still, many are uncomfortable using questions as a means of converting lectures to dialogues. Here are the answers to some of the most common questions about questions.

• **Is it better to call on participants by name or ask "overhead questions" and hope for volunteers?**

If you are trying to create a free flow of conversation and dialogue between learners and instructor, then it's better not to call on individuals

When they think that they know the answers, people are difficult to guide. When they know that they don't know, people find their own way.

– Lao Tzu, *Tao Te Ching.*

by name. Naming a respondent in advance can have several negative effects.

- The person may be embarrassed.
- Someone else may be better qualified to answer and thus be of greater benefit to the group.
- Others may feel that they are "off the hook" and may not think through their own answers.
- The climate may become one of classroom recitation, a "parent-to-child" series of transactions in which the instructor plays the role of judge.

An effective teacher can call on participants by name without encountering any of those negative side effects. One way is to let a person know why you're calling on her or him in particular. Example: Sandy, I know you've had some experience with this problem at your location. What do you think about this?

The danger of hoping for volunteers, of course, is that you may get none – or that the same people will respond, leaving the silent majority behind, not contributing and perhaps even resentful.

- **How do you get learners involved who never volunteer? What about that silent majority who see learning as a passive activity – a spectator sport?**

The much-cited 20/80 ratio probably applies to classroom behavior as well as to so many other phenomena. Namely, 80 percent of volunteered responses come from 20 percent of the learners. In a class of twenty people, the same three or four people may be answering all the time. Since people learn best by being actively involved, you want everyone to respond. How can you accomplish that?

Listen to what participants are saying. Focus on their concerns rather than your own. Effective listening entails a constant, conscious effort. Don't be thinking ahead while the participant is speaking.

– Charlene Reiss quoted in *Training* magazine.

There are many ways. After you've posed a question, have people turn to their neighbors and respond to them. On short answers, have each person write his or her response on notepaper, then discuss the responses. On polarized issues (on which the responses are yes/no, more/less, and so forth), ask for a show of hands for each response. Once you've broken the ice with such techniques, learners will be more willing to volunteer.

- **Is it a good idea to repeat participants' questions to make sure everybody understood?**

In general, yes, although repeating every question can become tiresome. Most questions shouldn't need repeating. But if the question was not worded clearly, was spoken too softly for everyone to hear, or came "out of the blue," then it may be a good idea to repeat it.

- **How should I deal with someone who has just given me a wrong answer, especially if the person has rank or status in the group? I'm thinking of the regional manager attending a local management seminar, or someone who's the in-house expert on the topic.**

There are two issues here. First, those with rank or status have no corner on the market when it comes to intelligence or understanding. Everyone in your class is entitled to make mistakes and have misconceptions. By the same token, everyone is entitled to respect; it is the instructor's job to "save face" for everyone.

If someone provides a wrong answer, it may be an indication that others are having difficulty. It's not likely that you picked the only person who did not understand. You may want to turn to the group after a wrong answer and ask, "How do the rest of you feel about Jackie's response? Is your own answer similar?" Such neutral wording will let you know how widespread the problem is, and may get another person who has an acceptable answer to explain the reasoning behind it to Jackie and anyone else who is having trouble. That relieves you from always being the one to correct wrong answers and gets your trainees to view one another as resources.

- **Sometimes I just don't understand an answer enough to know whether it's right. What should I do in such cases?**

You have several options.
- Tell the respondent that you don't understand what she or he is saying; ask the person to word it differently.
- If you think you understand some of what the trainee is saying, try restating it. The respondent will step in with clarification as needed.
- Ask the rest of the group for help: "Do all of you understand Thomas's response? I'm not sure I do. Can someone interpret it for me?"

- **What if someone takes forever to answer, is repetitive, rambling, or has trouble organizing his or her thoughts?**

Allow a reasonable time to organize an answer. If you see that the person is in trouble and that you're wasting group time, you may want to interrupt and summarize: "Let me see, Chris, if I understand what you're saying. You feel that ..." If you are at a loss to understand Chris well enough to attempt a summary, you may want to ask the group, "Can someone summarize Chris's response?" Or, you might simply interrupt, thank Chris, and say, "I'd like to get answers from several people on this question, since it's a difficult one."

- **What if no one answers my question?**

Let's examine some of the possible reasons.

- The question may have been so obvious or simple that no one wants to look like the class idiot by answering it.
- You may not have broken the ice yet, in which case you may want to try some of the techniques discussed earlier in this section.
- It's possible that no one knows the answer, in which case the question was premature or your instruction was inadequate.
- Perhaps no one understood the question. You might say, "Do you understand what I'm asking?" Ask trainees why this question seems to be giving them trouble. Or try rephrasing the question, which gives them new wording and additional time to think through the answer.

- **How should I deal with a learner who asks irrelevant questions that interfere with the flow of my instruction?**

If a question can be answered in a sentence or so, it might be easier to deal with the question rather than with the disruptive behavior. If the questions are making it hard for the other participants and you to keep on track, you might say, "I'm not sure how your question relates to the point we've been discussing ... Can you make the link for us?" This gives the person a chance to explain the relevance or graciously drop the question altogether.

- **What if a learner asks a question that is irrelevant but of great interest to the group, or a question that will be addressed later in the course but that is premature at this point?**

Sometimes a learner's question may be irrelevant or disruptive to you but of interest to the group (for example, a gripe they all have or a hidden agenda that is now exposed). At the beginning of the session, you might tape a sheet of flip-chart paper to the wall and give it the heading, "To be taken up later" or "Things to do."

As people ask questions that you'll be dealing with in subsequent sessions, you can write reminder notes for all to see. Sometimes participants bring up questions of a policy nature that you'll want to check with someone in authority before answering. The chart buys you time to do so.

If you've shared the schedule and the course objectives with the participants in advance, you're less likely to get irrelevant or premature questions. When you do, you can simply refer to the posted schedule or to the objectives.

THINGS TO DO:

-
-
-
-

- **If no one else answers, is there anything wrong with me answering my own question?**

If you asked the question to test understanding or to get the group's input, you're defeating your purpose by answering it yourself. Learners' failure to answer is a symptom, and you should try to analyze the problem underlying it. Was your question understood? Was it relevant? Do they know the answer?

Many teachers feel embarrassed if no one answers within a few seconds. You may have to wait five to ten seconds for an answer, especially to a complex question. Rephrase it to increase understanding of what you want. This also gives participants more time to think through their answers. If no one volunteers, ask trainees to turn to their neighbors and discuss their answers. You can then circulate, listening in on a half-dozen answers to find out where the group had trouble with your initial question.

- **What if I don't know the answer to a question? Doesn't that cause a loss of credibility?**

You'll lose more credibility by trying to bluff an answer than by stating that you don't know it but will try to find out before the next class. You might ask the group if anyone knows the answer. It's far more important to be a good facilitator than to be the one with all the answers.

- **How should I deal with someone who asks a question that is really a statement of opinion?**

One of the most common ways a participant will try to make a point is by asking a question. Such questions often begin with wording like, "Don't you think that the best way to ...." When you recognize that someone is really expressing an opinion or making a point, it's a good idea to throw it back to her or him: "That's a good question, Lee. What do you think?" In short, give the trainee the chance to make the point. Don't take it away by answering the question yourself or by throwing it to the group.

- **What if someone asks a question about something I covered ten minutes earlier? Should I take the time to answer?**

That depends. You might acknowledge for the group's benefit that you discussed the subject earlier, and reiterate the question. Ask if anyone else is having trouble. If no one is, you have a good reason to suggest that the learner see you during the break. Of course, if the question can be answered in half a minute or so, it's easier to do so and not make an issue of it.

There are some questions Donald Fairbairn calls "the seven deadly sins."[5] You'll probably recognize them from your own experience; they all seem legitimate, but not all challenge adult learners to think. These examples from my wine-appreciation course illustrate the seven types.

1. Factual and yes-no questions

Name three wine districts in Burgundy.

Which grape variety is legally permitted for the making of French Chablis?

This is probably the most common question type; unfortunately, it relegates learners to guessing and reciting. To reveal understanding, rephrase the question: If a customer asked you to explain the difference between a French and a Californian Chablis, what would you say?

2. Overlaid or multiple questions

Which two districts produce more *vin ordinaire* than any other and how much of it is turned into industrial alcohol?

This question asks for too much at once and confuses the listener. Even someone with the correct information can easily get muddled trying to respond to both issues. And if the question were divided into two separate ones, it still doesn't require more than the reciting of facts. How about a rephrasing that asks for a sifting of facts and an informed opinion: Why do you think so much wine ends up as industrial alcohol?

3. Ambiguous questions

Which wines are the best for everyday consumption?

Which are better, corks or screw caps?

Similar to the previous type, these questions confuse by being unclear. When asking for opinions and judgments, we must also provide criteria for such assessments. How about: What are the advantages of a screw cap from a consumer's point of view?

4. Chorus response questions

OK class, name the eleven German wine-growing regions, from the largest one down.

How do we pronounce the place name on this label?

No real harm is done, but such questions hardly challenge anyone to think, only to recite in the midst of other voices.

5. Leading questions

Which one is likely to be more expensive, a regional blend or a wine bottled by a château?

Watch me pull this cork. It doesn't matter whether I first remove the capsule, does it?

Objection, Your Honor, my learned friend is leading the witness. If you really want to determine what someone does or does not know, ask them! Otherwise, expect obliging replies that prove little in terms of individual understanding. They may also be seen as condescending by some and work against the positive effect of question-asking.

6. Ambush questions

The wine maker determines potential alcohol content by dividing the amount of grape sugar ... by what?

These start out as statements and suddenly become questions, catching participants off-guard. The disconcerting aspect of such questions is their sudden appearance when least expected. One moment participants listen passively to an explanation, the next they are expected to participate. It's much better to provide the explanation first and then, distinctly separately, pose the question.

7. Teacher-pleasing questions

What are we going to talk about tonight?

Who knows why I have selected these wines for tonight's tasting?

Some would argue that such questions, similar to most of the above, cause no harm. Perhaps. But adult education should be about making students think. Asking questions affords precious opportunities to detect areas of confusion and to flush out misunderstanding. Answering them provides participants with a clear sense of progress and accomplishment.

- **What if participants don't accept my answer and are fighting it? This often happens when I'm teaching company policy or procedures.**

Don't take sides by either defending or knocking the organization. Simply acknowledge that what you're explaining may not be popular, but that it is the way things are. If you know in advance that you'll be facing resistance, it's good to have the responsible persons there to explain and sell the new things you're teaching. You may jeopardize your effectiveness as an instructor if you question or defend your content. If the answer that is being resisted is not a matter of policy or procedure, you might try asking for help from the group. "Has anyone tried the technique I'm describing? What's been your experience?" Or, you may be able to relate a personal experience in which you found it useful to do what you just described in your answer.

In certain types of courses, you may want to state at the start that some of the suggestions and answers you'll be sharing won't be appropriate or acceptable to everyone. It is the job of each learner to select what is relevant and reject what isn't. Once you've said that, you can easily deal with participants who are fighting you: simply point out that if your answer isn't relevant, they shouldn't act on it.

CLASSIC CONCEPT

The inquiry method

The teacher's attitudes and beliefs have a strong influence on the composition of the learning environment, write Neil Postman and Charles Weingartner.[6] Their six principles show how to create a climate of inquiry in your classroom.

- *Principle #1: Rarely tell students what you think they ought to know. Telling as the main mode of instructing deprives the learner of the excitement and opportunity of self-directed and powerful learning.*

- *Principle #2: Use questioning as your major method of interacting. Rather than trying to seduce participants into reciting what you (or some other authority) consider the right answers,* use questions as instruments that can open minds to unexpected possibilities.

- *Principle #3: Generally, don't accept a single statement as an answer to a question – not because you prefer right answers, but because too often the "right answer" only serves to discourage further thought.*

- *Principle #4: Encourage student-student interaction as opposed to teacher-student interaction. Aim to minimize your role as the sole arbiter of what is acceptable and what is not.*

- *Principle #5: Rarely sum up the position taken by a participant. Instead, see learning as a process, not a finished product. There's a danger that your* "closures" will deter others from developing and expressing further thought.

- *Principle #6: Measure your own success in terms of behavioral changes in the learners. Do this by observing the frequency with which they ask questions; the increase in relevance of their questions; the frequency and conviction of their challenges to statements by others, yourself, or the text. Look also at their willingness to modify their positions when new data warrants it; their increased ability to observe, classify, generalize, and apply the results in an original way.*

10

Flexing learning styles

What would happen if in your workshop "not knowing" and "not understanding" were considered honorable behaviors?

"As a result of our hereditary equipment, our life experience, and the demands of our present environment, most people develop learning styles that emphasize some learning abilities over others," writes educational psychologist David Kolb. He and his research colleagues have developed the experiential learning model and the Learning Style Inventory.[1]

The theory

Kolb makes three assumptions about experiential learning. First, the experiential learning cycle occurs continuously and a learner repeatedly tests concepts in daily experiences in order to confirm or modify them as a result of reflection on the experience. Therefore, all learning becomes relearning and all education, reeducation.

Second, Kolb believes the direction learning takes is governed by a person's needs and goals. We seek experiences that are related to our goals, interpret them in the light of these goals, and form concepts (and test the implication of these concepts) that are relevant to our felt needs and goals. Therefore, when educational objectives are unclear, the process of learning is erratic and inefficient.

Third, since the individual learning process is directed by goals and needs, learning styles become highly individual in both direction and process.

Each person develops a personal learning style that has weak and strong points. We may be ready to jump into new experiences, but fail to observe the lessons to be learned. We may be good at forming theoretical concepts, but fail to test their validity. The ability to analyze learning styles can be useful – or even crucial – to those involved in a variety of educational fields, including course design, personalized coaching, team building, and personal development.

Four learning styles

Several theorists have developed instruments that purport to assess an individual's unique style.[2] Kolb's Learning Style Inventory (LSI) is probably the most widely used device; it helps to identify a person's preference for certain learning behavior, grouping the behavior into four statistically different styles.

- **Converger.** People who rate high on this style do best in activities that require the practical application of ideas. As they focus on specific problems, they organize knowledge through hypothetical deductive reasoning. Research has shown Convergers to be relatively unemotional, preferring to work with things rather than people, and having narrow technical interests, generally choosing to specialize in engineering and physical sciences.

- **Diverger.** Persons with this as their preferred style draw on imaginative aptitude and the ability to view complex situations from many perspectives. A Diverger performs well in brainstorming sessions and tends to be interested in people. With broad cultural interests – often specializing in the arts – counselors, personnel managers, and sociologists tend to have this as their preferred style.

- **Assimilator.** Persons with this as their preferred style excel in the creation of theoretical models and inductive reasoning. Although concerned with the practical use of theories, they consider it more important that the theory be logically sound; and if the theory does not fit the "facts," then they must be reexamined. This learning style is more characteristic of persons in the theoretical sciences and mathematics than the applied sciences.

- **Accommodator.** The strength of the Accommodator style lies in doing things and getting fully involved in new experiences. Quite the opposite of the Assimilator, this person excels in situations calling for theory application to specific circumstances; but if a plan or theoretical explanation does not fit the situation, the Accommodator will discard it. Problems are approached in an intuitive, trial-and-error manner. The Accommodator is at ease with people and often found in action-oriented jobs in business, marketing, or sales.

A word of caution

Many researchers, David Kolb included, warn against the use of any self-reporting instruments for the categorization of individual styles.[3] Neat classifications have their attractions, but no instrument is

We are all teachers, and what we teach is what we need to learn, and so we teach it over and over again until we learn it.

– A principle of A Course in Miracles.

absolutely reliable. It is important not to typecast people into one style. Most people operate with a combination of styles, depending on circumstances. However, we can make good use of test scores as indicators of preferred style.

Practical applications

If we want to find out how learners differ from each other, we usually rely on common sense, intuition, feedback from participants, and consultations with colleagues. However, learning-style data offers some interesting possibilities.

- Team-building tool
Instruments can be used as projective devices during trouble-shooting and team-building sessions. Instead of relying on the scores, use individual survey questions as discussion starters and to address interpersonal conflicts.

- Ice-breaker
To draw attention to individual differences, use a learning styles inventory as a warmup activity. Right from the start, the focus is on learning, on styles, and on ways each person can contribute to the group.

- Part of a needs analysis
Consider sending an instrument to potential participants and incorporate the results in the course design. Ask respondents also to indicate their preference for types of learning activities (rate your favorite classroom activities on a scale from one to five: lecture, discussions, individual projects, etc.).

- Aid to course planning
You can use individual or averaged group scores to custom-tailor certain learning activities for groups of like-minded participants. Or you can deliberately mismatch individuals with activities that will cause them to "stretch" their underdeveloped styles.

Our challenge

We can safely say that different people prefer to learn in different ways. Adult educators must design learning activities in which participants can develop a full range of learning styles.

Homines, dum docent, discunt – We learn while we teach.
– Seneca, Roman philosopher.

The experiential learning cycle

David Kolb, a developmental psychologist, suggests we look at adult learning as an experiential process. According to Kolb, learning is a four-stage cycle.[4]

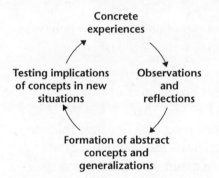

To be fully effective, a learner must develop four interrelated abilities. The teacher's job is to provide conditions that enable learners to ...

- become fully involved in an experience
- observe and reflect on the experience from many perspectives
- create concepts to integrate these observations into logically sound theories
- use these theories to make decisions and solve problems

To illustrate Kolb's model, let's follow a part-time student enroled in a criminology course through the stages of a project.

• Concrete experience.

As her task, she arranged to spend "A Day in the Life" of a homeless person. During the experience, she kept a written journal, interviewed street people on tape, and captured her impressions with quick pencil sketches.

• Observation and reflection.

The next morning, she reviewed her notes with the help of reflective questions provided by the teacher. (What happened? Describe five specific events that illustrate the life of a street person. What was your biggest surprise? How did you feel when you went home – to your own bed?)

• Conceptualization and generalization.

She subsequently met with a support group comprised of fellow students with similar experiences. Using a debriefing sheet previously designed in class, they shared their experiences and began to make connections between their field experience and theoretical materials. (How does your experience support or contradict your concepts of crime and poverty? Based on your experience, to what extent are the needs of your population understood and provided for by civic authorities?)

• Testing implications in a new situation.

On a subsequent field visit, she met with a social planner for the city to find out about services currently provided. Having learned about staffing and budget restraints, she met with her teacher with an idea for a new experience. She wanted to sound out several street people about the possibilities of forming a self-help group. The teacher pointed out relevant literature on the topic and suggested that the student meet with experienced street workers and members of a special policing unit in the downtown area.

And so a new concrete experience began ...

11 Observing group behavior

Teaching is reminding
others that they know
just as well as you.

– Richard Bach in
Illusions: The
Adventures of a
Reluctant Messiah.

When working on group assignments, people tend to behave in one of three patterns. One type of behavior helps the group to accomplish its assigned task; another serves to create cooperation and support; the third is focused on individual needs.

If you plan to utilize small-group activities, reserve some time up front to discuss these behaviors. Ideally, schedule this session early in the program, before anyone has had much opportunity to display any of these behaviors. People are much more likely to consider your comments if the slate is still clean. Your group probably has a few behaviors to add to the list and may want to change some of the labels and descriptions.

They may also agree to your suggestion to have one or two members act as observers during the next group task. Ask them to use the observation sheet and, after a suitable interval, report back to the group on what behaviors are most prominent. Keep the focus on what can be learned from the information, and assist members to monitor their own behavior.

With the help of a vocabulary to identify helpful behaviors, groups soon exhibit more helpful than hindering ones. Feel free to duplicate the list of predictable behaviors for discussion and observation. As participants become more experienced in teamwork, they begin to balance task and support roles, reducing their need for self-serving behaviors. Specific feedback helps to identify problem areas early and promotes those behaviors that help the group to function well. Once the vocabulary is familiar, suggest that individuals experiment with unfamiliar behavior in order to expand their repertoire.

By focusing on behavior instead of personalities, people are more willing to own up to their share in the group's struggle. The Personal Action form below can be used to make self-monitoring an explicit part of the learning process.

Personal Action Plan

Part I

Today, in addition to my customary behavior, I plan to practice at least one of the task-oriented and one of the group-building behaviors.

My chosen task-oriented behavior is _____.

I plan to practice such actions as:

_____
_____.

My chosen group-building behavior is _____.

I plan to practice such actions as:

_____
_____.

To assist me in this undertaking, I have teamed up with

_____(insert partner's name).

Together we'll share our action plan at the outset, agree to keep an eye on each other during the morning, and spend some time afterwards to debrief.

Agreed _____

Date and time _____

Part II
to be completed after the debriefing

As a result of the feedback I have received from my partner, I intend to practice the following group behavior

... during the next session in class

_____
_____.

... when I meet with my group back home

_____
_____.

Frequently check the pulse of the group. For example, if you sense that a discussion is running out of steam, ask for a show of hands of those who wish to continue for, say, ten more minutes. With this data, you and the group can decide how to proceed. You may also unearth a reason for the slow-down.

– David Quinlivan-Hall is co-author of *In Search of Solutions: Sixty Ways to Guide Your Problem-solving Group.*

Predictable group behaviors

An individual's behavior in a group can be viewed in terms of its function. A person saying or doing something that concerns the content and purpose of the discussion displays *task behavior*. Someone inviting a silent neighbor to speak up is engaging in *group-building behavior*. Actions aimed at satisfying personal instead of group needs are *self-oriented behaviors*.[1]

As your group becomes more experienced, you will find that behavior is increasingly focused on task and group-building functions. You can support this by soliciting feedback from observers, making appropriate comments, steering the discussion to the group process, and by encouraging individuals to monitor their own behavior.

Task-oriented behaviors

- *Initiating:* propose tasks or goals, define group problems, suggest a procedure or idea. Examples: "A good place for us to start would be to agree exactly what the problem is" or "I suggest we go around the group and find out what experience each of us has had with a similar problem."

- *Information or opinion-seeking:* request facts, ask for suggestions or ideas. Examples: "Dale, you work with this stuff all the time, what do you think we ought to do next?" or "Pam, you studied law – what are the rules on this?"

- *Information or opinion-giving:* offer facts, state beliefs, give suggestions or ideas. Examples: "There are two routes open to us ..." or "May I suggest we do a short brainstorming session to get our ideas on paper?"

- *Clarifying or elaborating:* interpret or restate ideas and suggestions, clear up confusion, indicate alternatives before the group, give examples. Examples: "So you are proposing that we present this agreement to the voters in a referendum. Is that right, Chris?" or "That's one way of going. How about an alternative. What if we ..."

- *Summarizing:* pull together related ideas, restate suggestions after the group has discussed them, offer a decision for the group to accept or reject. Example: "Let's just have a look at the ideas on the flip chart. It seems to me that two are impossible to achieve, but that the rest deserve further exploration. Shall we delete the first two from the list?" or "We now have to decide which plan to concentrate on, is it A or B?"

- *Consensus-seeking:* check with the group to see how much agreement has been reached, or can possibly be reached. Examples: "In spite of our differences, we seem to all agree on one thing ...; is that correct?" or "What would it take for each of us to agree to clause 4?"

Group-building behaviors

- *Encouraging:* be responsive to others, accept contributions of others, give others an opportunity for recognition. Examples: "Interesting question, Sandy" or "The sub-committee gave us such clear choices."

- *Expressing group feeling:* sense feeling, mood, relationships within the group and share personal feelings with others. Examples: "It seems to me we are overwhelmed by the amount of information we have to deal with" or "I like the way we're pulling together as a team."

- *Harmonizing:* attempt to reconcile differences and reduce tension by giving people a chance to explore their differences. Examples: "This has always been a contentious issue. What is it, I wonder, that both sides have in common?" or "We have been talking at each other for quite a while. How about we take turns to speak and before anyone can respond, we have to restate what the other has said."

- *Compromising:* offer a compromise, admit an error, discipline yourself to maintain group cohesion even when your own idea or status is involved in a conflict. Examples: "You are right, I have been stubborn on that point. I am prepared to ..." or "That was my mistake. How about we ..."

- *Gate-keeping:* keep the channels of communication open and make it easy for others to participate. Examples: "Devon, we haven't heard from you in a while. What do you think about ..." or "Gee, I have been doing most of the talking. I'd really like to hear what each of you think about the situation."

Self-oriented behaviors

- *Blocking:* interfering with the process by rejecting ideas, taking a negative stance on all suggestions, arguing unduly, being pessimistic, refusing to cooperate.

- *Deserting:* withdrawing in some way: being indifferent, aloof, excessively formal, daydreaming, doodling, whispering to others, wandering off the subject.

- *Bulldozing:* struggling for status, boasting, criticizing, deflating ego or status of others.

- *Recognition-seeking:* attempting to get attention by boasting, or claiming long experience or great accomplishments.

Content + process

When observing group activities, a distinction can be made between content and process. Content refers to what the group is working on; process describes how it does so.

Stages in the life of a group

As groups of adult learners work together, they pass through successive stages of formal and informal relationships.[2] Attention to such development is important. For example, asking relative strangers to share personal information could result in an awkward silence, but that same group may quite easily disclose information later on. A new group may have difficulty completing a cooperative task until it has acquired experience in problem-solving.

Several researchers have developed theoretical models of the predictable stages in a group's life. I find such theories to be worthwhile reference points when observing and managing group activities. According to Will Schutz, individuals and groups want and express three needs: inclusion, control, and affection.[3] A learning group typically begins with the first, then moves through the second, and on to the third. However, these stages overlap and the cycle may reoccur several times before the course ends.

- Need for inclusion

How might these needs express themselves in the classroom? The beginning need for inclusion is triggered when the group first meets in the new setting. People wonder how they will fit in and what they have to do to be recognized and accepted. Very little academic or content work can be accomplished until these and related questions have been dealt with. Warmup activities and simple small-group tasks are ways you can assist participants to satisfy their initial need for inclusion. Through such activities, people begin to reveal themselves a little bit at a time, tackling increasingly risky tasks as their comfort level rises. Still, in every group, one or two people will be unable to meet their inclusion needs.

- Need for control

The second phase of group development touches on control issues. They become apparent, for instance, when you ask learners to share responsibility for the course and when the group struggles with deciding how decisions will be made. During this stage, each participant strives to establish a comfortable level of influence with the teacher and other members.

- Need for affection

The next issues members face are those of affection and closeness. Natural affinities in the group may affect who supports whom during discussions, and how project teams are formed. Compatible groups, says Schutz, have members who complement one another's needs. That's why some groups seem to click, while others stumble and struggle. By anticipating these needs, perhaps mentioning them as legitimate and natural occurrences, you can assist in the development of individual and group competence and cohesion.

12

Rallying learning circles

Ask the same question of several people. Don't stop after the first answer, even if it is correct. Otherwise, certain people will do all the talking and others will remain quiet.

This technique comes in handy when you want to unearth opinions and feelings about a topic. It makes for more evenly distributed participation and acknowledges everyone's contribution. Use it at the start of a discussion to see what everyone brings to the table. Use it equally well as part of a lecture to measure comprehension and to flush out points of contention. Circles are helpful to get people to share previous experiences, recall good/bad memories, and describe feelings associated with a topic.

In essence, learning circles are an improvement on the question so often directed at no one in particular, "What do you think about X?" Instead of a broad floodlight, this technique spotlights each participant. The quality of responses tends to improve and most learners take a greater interest in the proceedings if their input has been sought in a meaningful manner. Whenever you ask for input, however, be prepared to incorporate it in subsequent discussion.

Learning circles are best used to ...
- gather quick statements about an issue from each participant
- focus the attention on the contribution of one person at a time
- demonstrate that all contributions are valued
- draw out reticent participators
- provide equal time and attention for each class member

Group size

This works best if there are fewer than twenty participants. In a larger class, two people could team up to prepare a joint response, or several circles could work independently. In such situations the outcome has to be summarized somehow (on flip-chart paper, or by an objective recorder) and brought before the whole group.

Time required

About thirty seconds per respondent.

Room setup

Ask participants to form a circle with their chairs. If that is not possible, ask people to situate themselves so they can see whoever is speaking at a given time.

How to proceed

1. Arrange seating.
If this is a new procedure, be clear with the instructions.

2. State a question.
Explain how you'd like participants to respond. The questions or issues may have been raised by students or the instructor.

3. Describe the process.
Explain that each person will take a turn to respond and that no comments are allowed during the initial round. Ask one person to start, then continue around the circle, until everyone has had an opportunity to respond. Begin the round with a different person each time you use this technique. Once the last person has responded, thank participants for their contributions, and summarize if you find that useful.

4. Model good listening behavior.
Use nonverbal encouragers to acknowledge and move along each speaker: nod, smile, make eye contact. If needed, keep the communications clear with clarifying and summarizing statements. If you can't fully understand what someone says, chances are others won't either. Clarify by saying something like, "I understand you to say that ... [summarize the speaker's main point] ... is that correct?"

Your listening and speaking behavior sets the norm for others. Avoid the temptation to evaluate or critique. Gently intervene if someone speaks out of turn or comments directly on another's contribution.

5. Ask for feedback.
How did we do? How did you like this activity? If we do it again, what changes would you recommend? Sometime after using a learning circle, ask participants about its usefulness. Be open to hear what's being said about the technique, your management, timing, and appropriateness. Listen for suggestions for improvement.

Variation: small circles

This is similar to learning circles, but instead of working with the entire class, you shift to small groups doing their own work. Each small group reports to the large one through a recorder. This technique can be used at various points of a session: everyone has the chance to get involved, and the technique requires little practice to bring results.

Small circles are best used to ...
- review material covered to this point
- concentrate learners' attention on a specific issue
- practice the use of peers' knowledge
- encourage learners to share their know-how
- develop group cooperation under time restraints

Group size

Use this whenever the class has more than twelve members. If there are fewer, use a learning circle.

Time required

Between eight and twenty minutes, depending on the complexity of the issue under consideration and the learners' familiarity with this approach.

Room setup

Enough space so that the class members can rearrange their chairs into small rounds. No writing materials are needed.

How to proceed

1. Form small groups.
State that the next task involves small-group work. Invite learners to form groups of about five to seven. Ask each group to shuffle so that they are equidistant from other circles.

2. Select recorders.
Request that groups select a recorder: it can be a volunteer or someone nominated by the group. Clarify the tasks for the recorder: jot down the group's comments and report to the whole class when asked to do so later. The recorder is definitely not the chairperson, but may briefly intervene if the group strays off the topic.

Don't assume that participants are competent in every instructional technique. The problem with some – brainstorming, for instance – is that they've been around for so long that we assume everyone knows what to do. It's a good idea to review the ground rules, and be ready to be a coach.

3. Appoint timekeepers.

Inexperienced groups will benefit from having a timekeeper. This participant takes on the additional job of letting the group know how much time is available at different stages of the discussion.

4. State the question.

Be very clear about the task you want the group to tackle. The technique works well with topics concerned with the learning process (How can we make best use of the discussion time?), as well as those addressing course content (What is your experience with ...?). Avoid simplistic questions and those that can be answered with a yes or no.

5. Set a time limit.

Write the task on the board for all to see and announce the available time in which to accomplish it. Such restraints add valuable structure to group activities. Should the work warrant an extension, you still have the option of adding time later.

6. Ensure understanding.

Too often groups get caught up in the excitement of the shuffling and socializing of group activities – until someone asks: what are we supposed to accomplish? Before sending the groups on their way, ensure everyone understands the task. One way to do this is to ask for one or two volunteers to restate the question. Another is to ask for clarification of the task from the group. Proceed only when the task is fully understood.

If you use time keepers, ask that they warn their group along the way ("Three minutes left") and towards the end ("You've got one minute left to complete the round"). For groups of six, you might start off with six minutes – one minute for each group member.

7. Brief the recorder.

This member, the only one who has to write, lists the contribution of each participant in the circle. A phrase or key point is enough for each response.

8. Propose a procedure.

New groups benefit from procedural guidelines at the outset. As groups mature and members become more familiar with your participatory mode, fewer directions are needed. You might say: "May I suggest you go clockwise around the group, beginning with the person

Occasionally, act stupid: "I may be a bit slow, could you explain ..." This will prompt the other person to think carefully and simplify the message. You'll also attract the group's attention and open the door to shared explorations.

> A. Everyone contributes; no one may skip a turn.
>
> B. Only when a speaker signals the end of a turn can the next person speak.
>
> C. Don't criticize or evaluate another's comment.
>
> D. It's okay to piggy-back – that is, use someone's comment as a springboard for further remarks.

who sits closest to the door" or "Start this round off with the person who spoke last during the previous discussion." Remind the group that equal participation demands tight management of time.

Posting the small-circles rules provides an easy reference point.

9. Start and stop the discussion.
Check the time and get the groups underway. The preliminaries, even with a new group, won't take longer than about five minutes. When the time has expired (with extra time if that's what it takes to get the job done), ask participants to turn their attention from the small groups back to the large group.

10. Invite recorders to report.
Ask them to report in point form on their group's deliberation. You may have to prompt some and restrain others. Stay focused on the previously posted task. Thank recorders and groups for their contributions. Open up for discussion or continue with the rest of the session.

13

Brewing brainstorms

Brainstorming is well suited to release and channel a group's collective creative energy. It invites uninhibited participation and often results in surprising ideas and solutions to old problems. Although most people seem to know the term, the first time you use brainstorming with a group, a careful explanation of the procedure is worth the extra time.

Brainstorming is best used to ...
- produce ideas about course content problems
- generate ideas arising from classroom process
- tap the collective creativity
- demonstrate the effect of synergy

Group size

This works well with about five to eight people. If your class is larger, two options are obvious: divide the large group into brainstorming groups of about six; or arrange one volunteer group in the middle of the room, with the remaining members as audience. In the second arrangement, leave an empty chair in the center group. Anyone from the audience can jump in and make a contribution at any time and then vacate the chair for someone else.

Time required

The activity continues until the group exhausts its initial idea pool, when no further ideas are forthcoming. It's hard to fix a time for this point to be reached, but five to fifteen minutes, plus time for evaluation and discussion, is the minimum requirement.

Room setup

Ask learners to shuffle their chairs so they face a mounted writing surface (chalk board, flip chart, or newsprint taped to a wall).

How to proceed

1. Arrange grouping and seating.

2. Post the target.
Examples: How can a manager avoid wasting time with telephone

---

**Case study: how brainstorming
was used to break the ice
and generate ideas.**

Brainstorming can be used in many ways for a number of goals. Here is an example in which it was used as both an icebreaker and idea-generator. The objective was to introduce a new administrative form to a group of government employees. For some this sounded like a dull topic; for all, it represented the threat of the unknown.

The trainer warmed the group to the topic by inviting them to brainstorm on the problems the new form was likely to present. After ten minutes even those who would otherwise have been silent realized they were in the thick of dealing with the issue. The trainer next handed out the new form and explained its features. The group then reviewed their flip-chart listing of potential problem areas and, with a little coaching, was able to see how these were dealt with on the new form. This paved the way for the new form to be accepted with open minds.

calls? How can we have better participation during class discussions? Note that either/or-questions (Should we do X or Y?) aren't suitable, nor are those inviting simplistic or factual answers (What are the staffing requirements for the night shift?). Brainstorming is best suited to issues calling for creative, wide-ranging possibilities.

3. Clarify the rules.
Be sure everyone is clear on the rules. Post them.

4. Assign recorders.
Ask someone with clear and quick printing ability to stand in front of the group and record *all* contributions as they are made. Suggest the recorder alternate colors to distinguish one comment from another. Allow no editing – although abbrev. are permissible. A visual record often sparks further contributions.

5. Call time.
Intervene when there seem to be sufficient ideas on the board or the group runs out of steam. Unblock the flow by asking participants to think of opposites, upside-downs, what-ifs, variations, add-ons.

6. Review and evaluate.
One strategy is to assist the group(s) in identifying the three ideas that seem the most practical and three that are the most outrageous. Play around with these to capture their combined appeal. Although the strict brainstorming rules are suspended, the second one (any idea is valid) still applies. Subgroups can be assigned the task of expanding on ideas that show promise.

- *Focus on quantity. Generate as many ideas as possible.*

- *Any idea is valid. Piggy-back on what others have said.*

- *Don't judge ideas. The crazier the better.*

- *Keep responses simple. Short and snappy is best.*

How to get the lead out

Synergy: "the combined effect of group members that exceeds the sum of their individual efforts." (Oxford Dictionary).

The problem with any popular technique is that people can become numb to its potential. Here are a few ideas on brainstorming to play with.

- *To limber up mentally, ask individuals to work alone for two minutes and prepare a list of possible ideas. This will provide each with something to contribute when the group gets started – or stuck.*

- *Similarly, teams of two could huddle and rapidly write down ideas on one sheet of paper. This huddling could occur at the outset or during a slump.*

- *Exchange recorders halfway through the proceedings, or when the group seems to run out of ideas. Any change in the group's makeup is likely to restart the flow.*

- *Try using two recorders working side-by-side to keep track of the ideas generated by a lively group. You could act as a traffic cop, directing words to one recorder,*

then another, to maintain the flow of ideas.

- *Use teams of two or three during the evaluation phase. Once the group identifies the ideas that are good candidates for "possible solutions," assign one to each subteam. Ask the small group to imagine obstacles and opportunities that would have to be dealt with to lead to an implementation.*

14 *Directing role-plays*

Role-playing involves experiential learning at its best. According to the *Concise Oxford Dictionary*, experience is the "actual observation of or practical acquaintance with facts or events." Experience can involve participants directly or vicariously; in role-playing there is no difference between the direct physical involvement or participation as an active observer. A well-managed role-play can be a powerful experience. We need only turn to reading and television to see how deeply felt vicarious experiences can be.[1]

By definition, role-playing involves one or more participants who act out a scenario, which is either scripted in advance or developed on the spot. Your task is that of casting director, stage manager, producer, and timekeeper. Participants become actors, audience, critics, and analysts. Even if you've never conducted a role-play, or remember previous ones with trepidation, I suggest you take advantage of this dynamic tool. Take a little leap of faith, then follow these step-by-step guidelines.

Role-play is best used to ...
- insert a slice of life into the classroom
- connect theory with everyday practice
- practice unfamiliar skills in a safe setting
- learn to appreciate contradictory viewpoints

Group size

Depending on the complexity of the play, you need two or more players. All others are designated observers; they either watch or are assigned witnessing functions. There is no limit to the size of the audience, but for larger groups, pay special attention to visibility, staging, and follow-up discussion.

Time required

A role-play can take as little as ten, but no longer than thirty minutes to complete. Preparation time depends on the complexity of the scenario; the duration of post-play discussion hinges on the issues and their relevance to the participants.

Experience is a hard teacher because she gives the test first, the lesson after.

– Vernon Sanders Law,
American baseball player.

Room setup

Everyone must be able to see and hear the role-players. The play itself may require some setup to simulate the situation being played out. A variation on the fishbowl arrangement will work well.

How to proceed

Successful role-plays run through four distinct phases: setting the stage, conducting the role-play, debriefing the action, and concluding the events. Thoughtful attention to each phase goes a long way towards a successful role-play.

1. Phase one: set the stage.

Start by explaining why you want to use a role-play and describe its benefits and process. To illustrate different ways of handling this phase, here are three approaches taken from a workshop on developing team leadership skills.

- Start with a *discussion* of problem situations linked with the topic under discussion. Example: I asked the group to think of common errors the chair can make at the start of a meeting. The ensuing discussion yielded a ranked list of errors. I then suggested that we role-play the opening phase of a meeting. One person took the role of chair, with six others acting as members of the committee.

- Alternatively, begin with a *lecturette,* outlining the theory that underlies the practice. Example: I drew attention to a chart of common meeting mistakes and we discussed a manager's obligations during the opening phase of a meeting. I then proposed a role-play with one of the group in the chair and four others as participants. They then experimented with the alternative approaches we had just discussed.

- Another opening can be created by viewing a *training film* depicting a problematic situation. Example: In this group we stopped the tape at crucial points so that role-players could take over the meeting and experiment with alternatives to what they had seen. A similar effect could have been achieved with a written *case study* as stimulus.

2. Phase two: direct the action.

Be specific in your instructions, answer questions about the process, but stay away from predicting possible outcomes of the role-play. Act confidently to help alleviate any anxiety that arises at the sound of the words "role play." A pragmatic approach tends to ease apprehension. Underscore that role-playing is less about acting, and more about learning by simulation.

Learning which involves the whole person of the learner, feelings as well as intellect, is the most lasting and pervasive.

– Carl Rogers

- Coach the players

Call for volunteers, or ask individuals you think will fit the part. There are usually enough people in any group willing to play; others take on the tasks of observers. Short written descriptions of characters and their scenario can be helpful; limit them to fifty words or less, just enough to sketch out the characters and their dilemma.

Elaborate scripts tend to restrain players' imaginations and will give you wooden performances instead of natural acting-out. Role-plays are meant to be a lively, lifelike enactment of some problematic circumstance.

- Brief the observers

Ask the nonplayers to find a spot from which they can best observe the play. Give them clear instructions on what to look for, what to write down, and what you hope to do with the collected data. For example, you can match observers with certain role-players and ask that they watch what that person says and does. Alternatively, observers can be assigned to report on player interaction – who says what to whom. The possibilities are plentiful: just make sure observers have a real function and don't see their role as busywork. Acting as observer offers valuable practice in observing, recording, and reporting. The fishbowl is a particularly useful room setup for such focused observations.

Six powerful interventions

1. *You can kick-start a role-play with a role reversal, where one player exchanges places with another. This can be particularly interesting in "us against them" situations where players stuck in one mode now have to see the world from the opposite viewpoint.*

2. *Halt the role-play and conduct a short coaching session with the player(s). You might ask, "How is the interview going for you?" or "Do you want to take a different approach? What would you like to do differently?" or "Let me make a suggestion: look at what we wrote on the flip chart earlier. Which of the alternative approaches might get you out of this jam? Please pick one, and just try it on for size." After such chats, players usually continue with new energy.*

3. *Ask players to exaggerate the situation. Instead of asking players to do it "the right way," instruct them to play the "wrong way" first, to overstate it until they get the feel for it. Example: In a workshop on interviewing techniques I said, "See if you can demonstrate an interviewer who is too preoccupied to really listen to the client." After a few minutes of that, I asked players to "become alert and apply as many active listening skills as may be appropriate."*

4. *Intervene with an aside, a technique frequently used in Shakespearean plays. When prompted, or at their own choosing, one player at a time may turn to the audience and share thoughts and emotions. One- or two-sentence asides can provide valuable clues to the observers and the other players without interrupting the flow of the play.*

5. *Tell everyone that it is perfectly acceptable for a player to stop the action at any time, to ask for directions, to say "I'm stuck," or to start over again. After all, role-playing is meant to be an opportunity to experiment!*

6. *With a more experienced group, suggest the method of alter ego. This involves seating a "coach" right behind one or more of the key players. As the play develops, such a coach assists by prompting the protagonist with key words or phrases. The player is free to pick up on the suggestion or pursue an independent course.*

Case #1: How to experiment with behaviors and achieve consensus on the "right way."

A group of trainers came together to experiment with ways to teach selling techniques to newly licensed real estate people. Aside from wanting to involve their learners more, these trainers also had a need for consensus on what to teach.

When they came to the topic of "cold calls," I suggested that two volunteers role-play a typical door-knocking situation. I briefed both to overplay, to do it wrong, but believable. After this hilarious opening, the group listed the flaws in the performance and generated "five rules for superior cold calling." Two fresh volunteers then replayed the scenario, this time by following the rules as much as they could. Their role-play took on a serious note and people later commented that it felt like the "real thing." Upon conclusion of the play, the rules list was edited and declared "correct" for future teaching sessions. Thus the role-play provided skills practice and consensus among a group of highly individualistic sales professionals.

- Your task is to concentrate on one participant *acting in the assigned role*. Sit so that you can face the person. Try to be unobtrusive.

- Note your observations on this sheet, and be prepared to report your findings at the end of the play.

- Quality will be more valuable than quantity. Record a few events in detail, so that you can report on who said what to whom, and what you saw happen because of that behavior.

1. Characterize the person's behavior *in the role*. Note a few specific behaviors and words to support your impression.

2. How did the person help or hinder the progress of the role-play?

3. If the person were to ask your advice on acting the part, what are your suggestions?

This is a sample only – adapt to suit your group's needs

- Begin the play
  For a while, stay out of the way and let the play proceed. There may be some initial hesitation until players get a feel for their role. If they get stuck, give them time to sort it out. If they become seriously stuck, make an intervention (see sidebar on page 66). Remember to jot down your own observations in preparation for the debriefing session.

- End the play
  After the play has taken its course, made a point, re-created a dilemma, or whatever you set out to achieve – call a stop. And how do you know when to stop and when to let it run for a little while longer? It may seem over, or the player may seem stuck, but with a little extra time or the right intervention, it could blossom into an unexpected surprise.

You must trust your intuition on this. If you sense a natural ending, but aren't quite sure what to do, step in, ask for a "time out," and consult the players. Ask if this is a good point to stop the play, or if a few more minutes would allow them to develop it further. Ask if they have gone as far as they can/wish/dare.

3. Phase three: debrief the events.

First, give each role-player an opportunity to report. Ask each person to describe the dilemma from their unique vantage point. This provides valuable inside information, and also helps players discharge any tension or discomfort they may have accumulated – especially important if a player had an unpopular part. Assist players to step out of their roles by suggesting they change seats and physically move away from their role.

Next, the observers report on what they saw and heard. This helps to develop their feedback skills. Ask them to comment separately on observed behaviors and their interpretation of them.

4. Phase four: wrap-up.

Assist participants to integrate role-play results with material previously discussed. Help them to generalize from the role-play to their real world. Ask "So what?" or, "What have you learned about ...?" Take the time now to thank the role-players for taking the risk, and perhaps make some light-hearted comments about what happened. Avoid identification of individuals with certain roles. Give feedback to the observers.

Case #2: How to provide insight into another's behavior and generate ideas for solving a problem.

During an in-house workshop for recently appointed managers, two participants mentioned their difficulty in having to share a key employee whose work affected both of their departments. I suggested a role-play to involve the group and to give the protagonists a chance to experiment with alternative behaviors.

We began with a situation that required them to cooperate on the contentious scheduling of the key employee. After a few minutes they began to feel the familiar heat, and I asked them to switch seats and continue the play in the other person's position. Some observers kept track of the dialogue, while others were assigned to record body language. When the role-play was stopped, both players expressed amazement at the similarity of frustration they had experienced in both roles. With the observers' input they were able to shift from their customary me-against-you to a new us-together-against-the-problem focus.

Ten tips for writing role-play scripts

1. Determine the purpose for the role-play and list the ability, awareness, or insight you hope participants will develop.

2. The value of a role-play depends on how successful you are in developing a scenario and role descriptions that suit the above objectives.

3. Outline the scenario. Decide on the name and nature of the simulated organization, and the number and type of roles. Sketch out the scenes of the role-play.

4. Use a plot line and props that are believable and consistent. Use realistic characters and events; for organizational scenarios, for example, use rules and procedures which might be used in the actual setting.

5. Provide relevant roles for participants. The best role-plays replicate situations with which they are familiar. Ask role-players to assume parts for which they have the necessary background. Adults like to see a job-related payoff in participating and acquiring skills.

6. Challenge participants. Ask them to generate alternatives as well as to choose among them. Train for the ability to propose options and criteria from which a decision will be made.

7. Check to see if the role-play fits the time available. Do participants have enough time to become familiar with the play, then analyze and generalize from it?

8. Give feedback. Emphasize positive features of each performance.

9. Test the role-play with a small group, possibly one that has had experience in experiential techniques. Analyze strengths and weaknesses and make necessary changes.

10. Solicit feedback from participants. Ask how relevant the role-play was in developing certain skills. Find out how realistic the scenario, the props, and instructions were.

CLASSIC CONCEPT

Body language

Apparently it is impossible for us not to communicate. Even when no words are exchanged, we communicate nonverbally, either through body movements, such as gestures, expressions, and stance; or by way of spatial relationships – the relative distance between people.

Albert Mehrabian reports on research into nonverbal behavior: the impact of facial expression is greatest (55%); next is the impact of the tone of voice (38%); and finally that of the words (7%).[2] Accordingly, if the facial expression or the tone of voice are inconsistent with the words, they will dominate and determine the impact of the total message.

The anthropologist Edward T. Hall coined the term "proxemics": the study of how we communicate through the use of space.[3] It deals with how far we stand from each other, how we arrange desk and visitor chairs, and how we respond to others coming into our space. Hall describes four distinct zones that North Americans unconsciously use as they interact: intimate distance, 0 to 18 inches; personal distance, 1/2 to 4 feet; social distance, 4 to 12 feet; and public distance, 20 feet and more. These spaces are largest in front of a person and smaller at the sides and back.

15

Teaching by demonstration

When it comes to teaching hands-on skills, the most reliable strategy involves a demonstration by the teacher, followed by supervised practice. Julia Child, television's *grande dame* of French cookery, is an outstanding demonstration teacher. Her shows come across as chatty and informal, but when carefully analyzed, they reveal meticulous planning and canny execution. Through hundreds of broadcasts, she has avoided "the deadly predictable sameness that shortens attention spans."[1] An equally impressive teacher is John Cleese – of *Fawlty Towers* and *A Fish called Wanda* fame – whose management training films are both entertaining and educational. Watching these two masters provides several teaching principles.

Describe the desired outcome

You need well-defined objectives that spell out what participants can expect to learn during the session. For instance, at the start of a show, Julia Child outlines her goals and displays the finished dish; viewers know exactly what she is aiming for.

Begin your own demonstration with a statement of objectives to describe the desired outcome in terms of *observable behavior*. State, for instance, that learners will able to "put the bridle on a horse" (riding course), "prune an established vine" (gardening course), or "prepare a Hollandaise sauce" (cooking course).

Since there are usually more wrong than right ways to perform a task, tell learners also the *acceptable standard* by which performances will be measured. Using our three examples, this could mean that "the bridle has to be fitted according to Pony Club rules," that the vines be "cut so that fruit spurs are spaced six inches apart with two buds on each new cane," and that the sauce must be "prepared in under two minutes, without curdling." Now teacher and learner have a clear depiction of what is expected.

Create a context

One trainer calls this the "zoom principle"[2] – giving the broad picture before going into details. John Cleese's training videos typically start with the whole story, explain why the job has to be done, how it fits into the whole picture, and only then teach the detailed steps.[3] In the riding-class example, the teacher might show pictures of incorrect and well-fitted bridles and, through questioning, prompt students to name the differences.

Identify the steps

Detailed steps, presented in a handout or wall chart, are ideal learning aids. They make it possible for participants to follow the demonstration and to check their own practice later. Such a published sequence also helps the teacher to avoid the "do as I say, not as I do" trap that can snare even the most seasoned practitioner.

Pace the sequence

Several techniques are available to spark interest and prepare the group for what is to come. The gardening teacher in our example could use the following techniques.

- Go *from the general to the specific* by asking participants to speculate on the reasons for regular pruning. This could then be followed by a demonstration of specific techniques.

- Start with the *first step first*, showing the untouched vine and ways to prune. Alternatively, she could demonstrate the *last step first*, beginning with a fully-pruned vine and, working backwards, show the cut-off shoots that resulted from the pruning.

- Ask learners to *experiment* before finding out the right way. For example, she could ask them to place twist-ties on unpruned vines to mark possible cuts. After a brief discussion, followed by the teacher's demonstration, learners would examine their markers and revise their intended cuts.

- Tell learners to validate their markers against correct ones shown on an *illustrated checklist*. They could also be asked to team up and check each other's handiwork. Only when confident, and with the teacher's go-ahead, would they finally put their pruning shears to work.

Watch me ... repeat ... then forget what you saw me do. Find your own way. Trust your body, it remembers.

– Chungliang Al Huang is a Tai Ji dancer, calligrapher, and philosophical entertainer. His books include *Quantum Soup* and *Embrace Tiger and Return to Mountain.*

Personalize the demonstration

Ensure each participant has an unobstructed view of the demonstration. Clarify how questions will be handled: as you go; after the demonstration; when asked for by you; or as posted on a flip chart or in a handout. Address people by name and maintain frequent eye contact. Synchronize your demonstration with the listed steps. Offer relevant background information as you proceed, but avoid getting sidetracked. Involve participants by inviting them to inspect the materials, hold tools, or manipulate equipment.

Another way to personalize is to establish a link to participants' lives outside the classroom. "Teachable moments" are created whenever instruction matches the immediate needs of learners.

Devise opportunities for practice

Whenever feasible, give participants an opportunity to practice the new skill. Even if that's not possible for all, at least have selected volunteers practice on behalf of the group. This way, others can observe, follow the steps on a checklist, and join in a discussion afterwards. Alternatively, arrange for small practice groups, with members taking turns performing the operation. Expensive, dangerous, or complicated practice may have to be simulated. Much of pilot training is done in simulators and the twist-ties in the vine pruning is an everyday example of simulated practice.

Act as coach and arrange for performance feedback

Supervise the practice and try to observe each participant at work. Learners can also team up and supervise each other, following a checklist or diagram and practicing until they are confident.

Feedback is most effective if given immediately after a certain action and if it specifically describes a behavior. Its value is enhanced if given in a helpful manner and perceived by the learner as aiding in skill acquisition. Provide participants with various measures of progress, and reward even approximations of the correct behavior.

Nudge learners toward flawless performance through one-on-one commentary, questioning, and assisting. Assist participants in helping each to learn. Simple feedback tools (see sample on page 73) and coaching guidelines will enhance cooperation. Ultimately, participants must be able to assess their own mastery of the demonstrated task.

What's in a name?
that which we call a rose,
By any other name would
smell as sweet.

– William Shakespeare,
Romeo and Juliet, Act II,
Scene 2.

Performance Feedback

Use this form to provide feedback during a practice session.

Name:

Task:

Date:

Place:

Coach:

Sequence of skills to be learned	Rating	Helpful comments
1. _____	1 2 3	_____
2. _____	1 2 3	_____
3. _____	1 2 3	_____
4. _____	1 2 3	_____
5. _____	1 2 3	_____

Key to ratings
1 = competent
2 = needs some more practice
3 = unsuccessful, needs further coaching

Facilitate transfer of learning

The real value of most skills training, and the justification for most adult-education efforts, lies in real-life application. This last stage in the demonstration-practice cycle must help learners to integrate newly acquired skills where they matter most. This could be on the job, at home, during leisure pursuits, or wherever the needs exist that brought people to your class in the first place. Several techniques are available.

- Build upon the new skill during subsequent practice sessions.

- Ask learners to reflect on how they can use the new skill outside the class. Have them contract with a partner to discuss its application in person or over the phone.

- Assign homework tasks that involve the use of the new skill, or invite participants to design their own.

- Suggest participants put their goals on paper and place it in a self-addressed envelope. Promise to mail it two months later as a reminder and reinforcer.

- Make time in a future session for reports on participants' use of the new skill.

Behavioral instruction

Robert Gagné describes conditions that make for effective instruction.[4] Sequence is not as important as the inclusion of as many components as possible. Here are his nine points with my commentary.

1. Gain and control attention.

Advertising people have a knack for this, as do entertainers and successful public speakers. They use gestures, examples, statistics, and dramatic statements of benefits and consequences to draw attention to themselves and their message.

2. Inform the learners of the expected outcome.

Most of us appreciate knowing where we are going, what's in it for us, and why we should make the effort. Tell participants what they can expect to gain from listening, participating, experimenting, and studying.

3. Stimulate recall of relevant prerequisites.

Connect new material with old, unfamiliar with commonplace. Examples: "Remember the last time you tried to get your partner to listen to you, but ended up frustrated?" or "Our previous discussion raised some points we didn't get to. I've written them on this flip chart so we can deal with them today."

4. Present new material.

Now that you have "primed the pump," continue the flow of learning by presenting new information, demonstrating a skill, or facilitating a discussion.

5. Offer guidance for learning.

Do whatever it takes to help participants learn. This book is filled with techniques, including small-group activities, individual projects, questioning, role-plays, and case studies.

6. Provide feedback.

Inform the learners yourself, expose them to appropriate models, or create situations that will yield the data, so that participants can gauge their progress.

7. Appraise performance.

Before moving to the new set of materials and experiences, learners should have a chance to measure themselves against some external standard. Techniques that can help them include models, tests, trials, experiments, reflection, and evaluation by self, peers, and experts.

8. Make transfer possible.

Adults don't learn for the teacher's sake, but for many reasons of their own – perhaps to upgrade their job performance, raise their academic standing, develop their hobby skills, improve their functioning as a parent, or enrich their enjoyment of life in general. Practice sessions in class and individual projects and assignments can help facilitate transfer.

9. Ensure retention.

To take hold, new attitudes, knowledge and skills need to be used and reinforced. Try ways of applying new data to familiar problems, draw connections between new and old, use methods that demand recall and retention.

16 *Inspiring participation*

There will always be some people who naturally participate and others who sit back and remain relatively silent. Both present a challenge: how to slow down the keen ones without offending and how to bring out the quiet ones without pressuring. Here are two games, Speedy Memo and Spend-a-Penny, that can easily be interjected whenever you wish to regulate the flow of participation.

Speedy Memo

This is a quick way to sort out any number of unspoken elements in a group. With only a minor interruption of the proceedings, it serves to clarify a fair measure of what's going on in the room. Everyone has a say and only minutes are required to gather and process the information.

Speedy Memo is best used to ...
- obtain quick feedback on opinions, facts and feelings
- bring personal comments to light – in confidence
- create an opportunity to find out learners' hidden needs
- pause for a midstream assessment
- conduct an informal opinion poll

Group size

This can be used with groups of any size. To save time during processing of responses, large groups may be broken into subgroups of five to seven to collect and announce their data.

Time required

Less than it would take for a coffee break, when some of these things would be discussed anyway – without the benefit of being analyzed or used.

Room setup

The existing one. Even in large lecture situations, subgroups can be formed by people briefly turning to those sitting behind them.

There are no wrong notes!

– David Darling, master cellist, composer, conductor, and teacher of improvisation. His CD recordings include *Cycles*, *River Notes*, *Amber*, and *Cello*.

How to proceed

1. Describe the process.

Ask participants to briefly pause and listen to an explanation of the speedy memo process. Explain what it is you want to know. Examples: What was the highlight of today's session? What part of the lecture warrants further exploration? How do you feel about the way this role-play is going – what should we do in the remaining ten minutes?

Of course, you'd only ask one question at a time, or, as in the last example, raise two related items. Write the question on the board to be absolutely clear.

2. Do it.

Ask each person to get a small piece of paper – something torn from a notebook or the corner of a handout will do.

Invite participants to respond with one or two words. They should be as concise as they possibly can. Suggest using a noun, an adjective, a verb, an exclamation: at most one telegram-style sentence.

Quickly collect the papers, mix them up, and ask one or two people to read them out loud. Now everyone knows what others are thinking and feeling.

3. Process the new data.

Respond to the message. This may be something you can do, or, more likely, something others can help with. If appropriate, engage the class in discussion on how to deal with the information.

Spend-a-Penny

Although simple, this can be a very effective technique to get everyone to participate in class activities. It can be quickly inserted at any time without detracting from the content of the session.

Spend-a-Penny is best used to ...
- encourage even the most timid learner to participate
- slow down frequent contributors without cutting them off
- demonstrate that everyone has equal rights and responsibilities
- shift the focus from content to process
- add a playful element – with a very functional purpose

Group size

This can be done with groups of any size.

Time required

Just enough to explain the rules and distribute tokens. From there, the class continues to work on the task at hand.

Case #1: How did I do?

Once I was sure that my presentation had bombed: participants had left in a sombre mood, no one had lingered behind. I was sure I had created more confusion than clarity. The next morning, before doing anything else, we used a Speedy Memo asking for a one-word description of my lecture. The responses surprised and humbled me: I was told that yes, my presentation had been incomplete, but, more importantly, thought-provoking. People recalled leaving the room in a pensive mood, not because of a job poorly done, but because I had got them thinking about the subject in a profound way. The fact that I showed such concern for their moods made quite an impression and furthered our development as a group, learners and teacher alike.

Materials needed

Three pennies (coins, poker chips, or any symbolic token) per person.

Room setup

Participants stay where they are.

How to proceed

1. Explain the purpose of the exercise.

By being brief you'll hardly lose the flow of what's been going on. Introduce this as a way to encourage and equalize participation. It is probably best to avoid singling out individual behavior you wish to remedy, but I have been known to say something like, "two or three people have been doing all the participating," or "the participation on this topic has been a bit lopsided this morning and I'd like to hear what the rest of you have to say."

2. Explain the activity.

Tell everyone to stay where they are. Distribute tokens, or simply ask participants to produce three coins.

3. Explain the rules.

Pennies can be spent during the ensuing session in the following manner. Every time a person speaks up, it costs a penny, which is placed in front of the speaker. Once all three are spent, the participant has used up his or her opportunities to participate and must remain quiet. This way everyone has equal opportunities.

4. Get on with it.

Engage participants in an activity that offers active participation, such as a discussion, demonstration, question-and-answer session, or case study. You may need to remind them of the basic rules, but people usually get into the swing of things.

5. Invite discussion on the activity.

Some time after using Spend-a-Penny, ask the group to comment on its usefulness and future use. This should not be a critique of the exercise, but an assessment of its effect on the level of involvement. Ask the group to think of ways everyone can ensure a more balanced participation. "Pennies" might become a code word for the group. If, for instance, a discussion becomes too one-sided, anyone could invoke the "equal-penny rule" as a reminder to let everyone have an equal share in the proceedings.

Case #2: Computing priorities

In the midst of a day-long workshop, I needed help in deciding where to go next. Our agenda still listed several points as important, yet we were running out of time. Several options lay before me. I could, for instance, exercise my teacher's prerogative and choose the items to cover. Or I could ask the group and spend precious time on a selection process. A show of hands with quick tallies next to the remaining items might have been the way to go, but because of the sensitive nature of the issues, anonymity was called for. A Speedy Memo soon yielded the top two items on the group's priority list.

How to slow down the fast ones

Spend-a-Penny is an effective way of handling the expert in the class who always has something to say and may prevent others from making a contribution. I have found that such frequent contributors, rather than being put off, respond positively. For some, it was a relief to sit back and let the others speak.

How to encourage the quiet ones

Those who usually sit back in relative silence find this an easy way to make contributions. Some have said with amazement that spending their pennies represented a change in their usual behavior: they got caught up in the play and found it easy to speak up. Not having to compete and being assured an equal voice can be quite liberating.

CLASSIC CONCEPT

Facilitating adult learning

Carl R. Rogers, psychologist and educator, proposes guidelines for the facilitation of learning which have become my creed.[1] Accordingly, I ...

... consider myself largely responsible for setting the initial mood or climate of a program.

... try to elicit and clarify the specific goals of individuals as well as the more general purposes of the group.

... rely on each participant's desire to implement those goals as the motivational force behind significant learning.

... organize and provide access to the widest possible range of resources for learning.

... regard myself as a flexible resource to be utilized by the group.

... aim to become a participant learner, a member of the group, expressing my views as an individual.

... take the initiative in sharing myself with the group – my feelings as well as thoughts – in ways which the others can take or leave.

... strive, frequently surprising and always humbling as it may be, to accept my own limitations as a facilitator of others' learning.

17

Studying cases

Case studies typically describe a sequence of events and challenge participants to come up with an analysis and recommendations. Working alone or in small teams, learners are asked to deal with one or more questions, from simple to complex. For instance: What happened here? Define the problem. How can the problem be resolved? What impact might the proposed solution have?

Case studies are traditionally presented in writing, but could also arise out of a training film which is stopped in mid-action. Potentially, case studies offer exciting opportunities to link theory and practice. To do that well, they have to be believable and challenging.

Why not write your own case studies? You are eminently qualified: you know the participants, their backgrounds, their practical experience, and you are familiar with the terminology and jargon of their field. You also have pretty clear expectations of how a case might contribute to everyone's learning efforts. All you need, it seems, are some tips on writing cases that capture the reader's imagination.[1]

Write in the form of a story

From children's fairy tales, teenage comics and adventure books, to adult novels, films, and television series, we are fascinated by well-told stories. A good case study must have a story-telling quality to it.

Give the characters real names

Instead of referring to the protagonists as Boss, Supervisor A, Irate Customer, Secretary, Department Head, Lab Technician, or even Dr. Brown or Sue White, be more adventurous. Give them interesting names: D'Arcy, Karline, Jean-Marie, Sebastian, Wolfgang. Or play with words: Fred B. Friendly, Jura Paine, Thorfie Thorfinson, Zyzzy Zazu.

Put words in the mouths of characters

When Red Riding Hood arrives at Grandma's house, she doesn't cry "Wolf" immediately; she puts Grandma through the interview. We all know that she's addressing a wolf in drag, but the dialogue adds much-loved suspense. So instead of writing that the manager asked her staff for details on the incident, report the interaction in realistic words. It might be something like: "Rollo, I just read the complaints log for last night. What a mess! What happened?"

Use realistic details

Use authentic terminology, everyday jargon, and convincing details to make the case study believable. In a case involving hotel operations, when receptionists worry that they may have to "walk" a guest, they mean that because of overbooking a guest will have to be sent to another hotel and given complimentary accommodation and transportation. When they calculate the number of registered guests, they speak of a "house count"; "walk-ins" are guests who came without prior reservation; and the general manager is the "GM."

Be descriptive

Appeal to readers' senses; make it easy for them to imagine what it was like: describe sounds, textures, and movements. Let's apply this to a line from a case study on emergency procedures. "At the time of the accident, the reception area was very busy."

A more vivid description does a much better job of conveying the drama of the case. "The digital clock showed 6:32. Kelly was alone at the desk while Chris was downstairs having dinner. The airport bus had just left, dropping off all kinds of people. Through the glass doors, the doorman could be seen helping four people out of their taxi. Kelly reached for the phone to ask Chris to come back early. Suddenly she heard a thundering bang, followed by a sharp cracking sound, and the noise of breaking glass. And then – a loud scream. She dropped everything and ran over to see what had happened."

Make the flow easy to follow

Present the events as they occurred. The previous paragraph describes the chronology of the incident from the staff's point of view. It sets the scene, then describes specific events and Kelly's action. Avoid the use of flashbacks.

If a little knowledge is dangerous, where is the man who has so much as to be out of danger?

– T.H. Huxley (1825-1895), English philosopher and critic.

Be complete and mysterious

Unless you specify that learners find supplementary information, the case study should contain all that's needed to proceed with the analysis. Information should be contained in the case description itself, or be provided in accompanying materials. The accident case above is accompanied by a copy of the hotel's emergency procedures manual. Depending on the experience level of the participants, a case study leaves room for interpretation and speculation.

Provide lead questions

Conclude the case study with questions or assignments that clarify the objective of the exercise. In our accident example, they are asked to meet in groups of three and assume the representative roles of management, union, and safety committee. They are then given two starting questions: How were the emergency procedures followed? How could our response capability be improved?

Acquire new knowledge whilst thinking over the old, and you may become a teacher of others.

– Confucius (K'ung Fo-tsu, c551-479 BC), founder of a philosophical system based on peace, order, humanity, wisdom, courage, and fidelity.

18

Inviting experts

I attribute the little I know to my not having been ashamed to ask for information, and to my rule of conversing with all description of [people] on those topics that form their own peculiar professions and pursuits.

– John Locke (1632-1704), English philosopher whose writings helped bring about the European Enlightenment period, also known as the Age of Reason.

There are points in any course when it makes sense to employ an outside expert to contribute timely information and valuable experience. But what's the best way to integrate guests into the program? Customarily, teachers make all arrangements and then hope that the guest brings content expertise *and* teaching ability. Course participants have little say in these arrangements and in the end may derive little benefit from the expert's input. A waste of time and talent? It doesn't have to be.

I suggest you involve the participants from initial planning to final event. Instead of bringing strangers together and praying they'll connect, take a pro-active approach and organize a debate format. It will reduce the pressure on the guest to cope with a strange environment and at the same time involve the whole group. Now everyone has a stake in making this event a success.

After all, you know your students and you probably have strong ideas of the guest's role in the overall course plan. This debate format leaves you in control of quality while taking full advantage of the expert's know-how. As the interviewer and moderator, you will be able to prompt the guest with questions, demonstrate interviewing techniques, and act as traffic control during the questions and answers.

Occasionally a guest is chosen to present a formal lecture or speech. In this situation, your function will be limited to introducing the speaker, possibly to moderating the question period, and to expressing appreciations at the end.

Expert presentation is best used to ...
- involve participants in every phase of a guest presentation
- work with novice guest speakers
- ensure that the guest's presentation fits into the course agenda
- ensure fruitful interaction between guest and class

Class size

As long as everyone can see and hear the guest, there's no limit to the class size. If you are counting on interaction between speaker and participants, then the group has to be small enough to allow that. If yours is a very large group (over twenty, say), you can use small buzz groups as a way of bringing audience and guest together.

Time required

Long enough for the guest to deliver the information and for your class to have the chance to raise issues, ask questions, or debate points made by the guest.

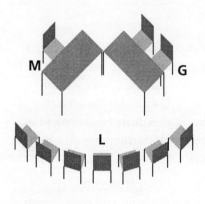

M = Moderator
G = Guest(s)
L = Learners

Room setup

Arrange the furniture in some way so that you and the guest face each other *and* the audience. You can easily add a chair or two to accommodate more than one guest.

How to proceed

1. Select potential guests.
If possible, involve your participants in the choosing. Be clear what function the guest is to fill to enhance the group's learning experience.

2. Meet with the guest.
Do this face-to-face if possible. Otherwise discuss things by phone or correspondence. I suggest you negotiate directly with one person to ensure you know who is coming. After all, you are trying to fit this expert into your course and you are acting on behalf of all participants to ensure you get the best. The potential guest, too, deserves a fair chance to make an informed decision. If possible, give the class a choice of speakers. Involving the participants in this phase will enhance the guest's contribution and class participation.

3. Arrange logistics.
Once you have the right guest or guests, confirm the details of date, start and finish time, pay, parking, security, and telephone contacts. Sort out who is responsible for audio-visual aids, duplication, and other support materials.

4. Work out a teaching plan.

Go over the details of the event and agree on a schedule of who does what and when. Discuss timing for start, breaks and finish, and when and how participants will get involved. Clarify your own role: explain that you'll be sitting with the guest at the front of the class, that you'll be acting as interviewer only to keep the discussion on topic, as moderator only during the question-and-answer session. Determine if any preparation or prior reading is required.

5. Prepare participants.

The guest session begins long before the expert arrives. If participants were involved in the initial decision, tell them why you are asking this guest to come and what can be expected. Prepare the class by brainstorming questions, assigning and discussing preparatory readings – anything you can do to "prime the pump." Explain the teaching plan for the session; describe what's expected of each participant. Ask for volunteers to introduce and thank the guest.

6. Manage the event.

When the day arrives, arrange furniture (get help from the participants), introduce the panelists, act as interviewer to get the guest going and on topic, and eventually be the moderator to direct the interactions. Try not to dominate the discussion; instead, do everything possible to bring out the best in your guest *and* boost learning opportunities for everyone involved.

Variations

Class members as expert panelists

Right from the start of a course, assign participants the job of paying special attention to given course material in order to develop a special expertise. Later on, arrange panel discussions among these "experts." Example: in a philosophy course, participants took on the roles of dinner guests at Plato's *Symposium* and argued an issue as they imagined their characters might have. In another case, management students discussed the issue of quality control in hotel services from the perspective of manager, desk clerk, and frequent guest. In both situations, the audience initially observed the discussion, then interacted by quizzing the experts on points that had been raised by the staged discussion. The instructor acted as moderator, continually bringing it back to the objectives for the session and away from personalities and preoccupations with acted roles.

Trusting the other is to let go; it includes an element of risk and a leap into the unknown, which takes courage.

– Milton Mayeroff,
 On Caring.

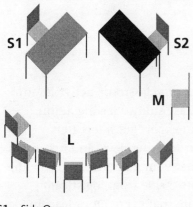

S1 = Side One
S2 = Side Two
M = Moderator
L = Learners

Arguing different sides of a controversy

This is a variation on the panel debate. It works well when your topic involves strongly held views on controversial issues. During the debate, equal time is given to each side of the argument. Use this technique in an impromptu way as an issue arises, or plan – even rehearse – it as part of your agenda. The room setup is similar to that for an expert debate. To heighten the drama, seat the opponents face-to-face with only a table to separate them. The moderator, either the teacher or an experienced participant, sits off to the side or between the arguing parties.

Example: In a course on environmental issues, we frequently ran into situations where people held strong personal views. Although the group agreed on most fundamental issues, when it came to matters concerned with individual versus public rights, tempers flared. A debate format allowed the airing of opposing viewpoints and gave each side a chance to hear and learn from the other. Coupled with the variation below, this technique frequently led to new insights and softening of rigid postures.

Hearing opposing views

After the first round of debate, ask the opposing sides to switch positions with each other and continue the discussion. This gives each person an appreciation of the other's position.

It is in fact nothing short of a miracle that the modern methods of instruction have not yet entirely strangled the holy curiosity of inquiry; for this delicate plant, aside from stimulation, stands mainly in need of freedom; without this it goes to wrack and ruin without fail.

– Albert Einstein

19

Learning outside the classroom

Believe one who knows. You will find something greater in woods than in books. Trees and stones will teach you that which you can never learn from masters.

– St. Bernard of Clairvaux (1090-1153), French theologian and mystic who founded sixty-eight religious houses and acted as adviser to popes and kings.

Occasionally a dose of reality is needed to put classroom activities into context. You can do this by discussing a case study, viewing a film, reading relevant articles, or by bringing in expert guest lecturers. Alternately, you can send participants out for interviews and first-hand observations. They can go as a group under your guidance, or individually, having made their own arrangements. Aside from logistical responsibilities, your main task is to ensure that every bit of learning is first extracted and then connected to the rest of the course of study.

A field trip is best used to ...
- provide a first-hand view of a process, procedure, event, or location that cannot be brought to the classroom in a better way
- establish connections between classroom instruction and real-life practice
- collect impressions and information for classroom analysis and discussion

Group size

If you plan to go as a group, keep the party to under ten participants for every guide. In larger groups, people tend to form smaller ones, where they end up with their own conversations, trying to make some sense of what's going on around them. If your group is larger, break it into subgroups. Assign a guide to each group, or if that is not possible, begin the tour with an assembly in a place where everyone can hear the speaker, then send participants in small groups, with a printed guide or observation sheet. Agree on a time for all to reconvene and conduct a question-and-answer session to tie up loose ends.

Time required

First, allow time to make the arrangements. Leave enough time to explain the goal of the visit to the class and to put the visit into a context: here's why we are going; this is what I'd like you to look for; here's what you are expected to bring back. Finally you need to count on travel time from one place to another. To eliminate loss of class time, persuade participants to travel on their own time, using their own transportation.

How to proceed

1. Make the arrangements.

Do this well in advance and confirm them in writing. Visit the site yourself. Discuss the planned sequence of events and walk over the proposed route. Confirm the name and title of the person who will be your host; find out who might be the alternate in case of unavoidable substitution.

2. Get to know your host.

Unless you will provide the expert guidance during the visit, get together with the person who will perform this function. Treat the guide as a guest speaker: you need to work together to make the visit educational, rather than social. Try to get to know the guide; describe your participants, their backgrounds and their expectations. Explain what your learners already know and where, in the overall scheme, this visit fits in.

3. Prepare the participants.

Brief the class by telling them about the site you plan to visit, why you are going there, and who will be there to meet them. The class as a whole can make a list of questions about the site.

4. Confirm directions, time, and place.

Make sure everyone knows where to go on the date of the visits, as well as other information: emergency telephone contact, rides, material to bring, dress.

5. Follow up.

After the visit (or during your next class meeting), discuss the trip, give additional information and relate it to the course.

Send a note of thanks to your host; there is always next season's group to think of.

If you want to learn about the universe, go and look towards the heavens. Don't bury your head in some poor Latin translation.

– Roger Bacon (1214-1292?) lived in Oxford and Paris as a Franciscan friar. He anticipated steam engines, aircrafts, and microscopes. Condemned by the church as a heretic, he was exiled for ten years, forbidden to teach and write.

Variation : Individual field project

Instead of taking the whole class on a guided tour, participants go on their own or in teams of two. Such a scheme is especially useful if the location and times for visits fall outside normal class hours. Carefully planned and integrated, projects provide personalized learning opportunities through observation, reflection, and reporting.

How to proceed

1. Establish a list of potential hosts.
Arrange for a list of potential hosts and leave it to each participant to arrange the details. If you state your criteria for what makes a suitable project site, students can find alternate placements to those on the list.

2. Prepare students for the project.
If this is a mandatory component of the course, participants need to be clear on what's expected. Discussions, handouts, and role-plays can help to prepare them to make contacts and to derive the greatest benefit from the project. A letter of introduction and observation forms can be made available as additional support. If a grade will be assigned, evaluation criteria must be agreed upon prior to the visit.

3. Debrief and integrate the project.
As with any experiential learning event, the debriefing is crucial. You can assist participants to identify key learning points by teaching them to recall details, reflect on events, and draw personal conclusions, making valuable connections between the abstract and the concrete.

The use of traveling is to regulate imagination by reality, and, instead of thinking how things may be, to see them as they are.

– Samuel Johnson (1709-84), English man of letters, critic, and lexicographer. After failing as a schoolmaster he supported himself by journalism and hack writing.

Case #1: Anatomy of a field trip

Once a year I offer a continuing education course on wines and spirits. Halfway through the course, when participants have theoretical knowledge of the wine-making process, we visit a winery.

Participants are involved in the planning decisions, but it is up to me to make initial contacts, visit the site beforehand, meet the wine maker, outline the course, describe participants' backgrounds, and explain our objectives. During my initial visit, I'm able to gather information on the operation and get to know our host. Arrangements are confirmed in writing. When the class meets just prior to the visit, we develop a list of questions students are curious about. Everyone makes their own travel arrangements, but maps, names, and phone numbers are exchanged to avoid lost sheep.

Once at the site, we begin in a meeting room where introductions are made and the day's plan is sketched out. Our host, the company's wine maker, then explains the production process by way of a flow chart. The subsequent tour more or less follows this outline, and we scramble through laboratory and loading docks, past refrigerated tanks and noisy bottling lines. Eventually, everyone reassembles for a tasting session and we are joined by the marketing manager. We use this time for questions and answers and after a brief stop in the winery's retail store, we depart.

Soon after the visit, a letter of thanks is signed by the participants and sent to our hosts. We also discuss points raised by the visit and the tasting. Occasionally, observed practices differ from those discussed in class or read in a book. Such details make for interesting discussions and serve to integrate theory and practice.

Case #2: Anatomy of an individual field project

We have used individual projects in several settings where groups would not be allowed. The hotel business is a good example. Managers don't want to see a horde of students traipse through lobby, restaurants, and guest rooms, yet they are hospitable and keen to show their properties off to newcomers. Individual projects have worked well with students in junior college programs, night classes, and people enrolled in distance education courses.

Students are asked to select their own hotel operation, to contact the owner or manager, and to arrange for a minimum of four hours "working" behind the front desk. They are given study guides that outline the learning goals and the reporting procedure. They also receive a letter from the course coordinator, explaining the project and expressing appreciation for any assistance. Beyond that, students proceed on their own.

Results have been positive. Participants have brought back reports that show how much they have learned; some came away with part-time job offers, others with the realization that this kind of work, after all, was not for them. In many instances course material was verified; in others, it was questioned by more confident students. Instructors and managers report that projects keep them on their toes and that students value their new industry contacts and the opportunity to make "cold calls" for interviews. They also returned with information and anecdotes that would contribute to everyone's classroom experience.

20 *Individualizing assignments*

Determine learners' prior educational experience. People's expectations are influenced by previous learning, especially childhood experiences. Some may need to learn how to learn, including how to take increased responsibility for their own learning.

Give me a fish and I can eat today; teach me to fish and I can provide for the rest of my life. Or so goes the saying. If you believe in developing self-directed learning skills, then delegate certain tasks to the participants. Such tasks are typically done outside class time, by individuals or teams, and may involve library research and assigned readings, in addition to writing and/or presentation components.

Adults have little tolerance for busywork and appreciate assignments that have high relevance to their personal needs, stretch their individual learning style, and constitute a legitimate course ingredient.

Individual assignments are best used to ...
- create self-teaching opportunities that recognize individual differences
- develop the skills necessary to search for data and analyze it critically
- reduce the teacher's function as primary information source
- complement information provided by the teacher and usual references
- develop supplementary reading lists

Time needed

Although the assignments are done outside class time, you need to create ways (and time) to integrate the material into the classroom activities.

How to proceed

1. Define topics.

2. Provide guidance.
Assist with access to information. Put participants in touch with specific literature pertaining to both content and process of the research. Make referrals with resource personnel, such as librarians, information officers, and faculty members.

3. Set a completion date and discuss consequences for late completion.

4. Plan how to make best use of the material being collected.

This can be done in a variety of ways, including annotated reading lists, abstracts of journal articles, executive summaries, book reports, and bulletin boards. Depending on your circumstances, information can be shared through oral report, electronic mail, visual display, or a number of print formats.

5. Ensure a good fit between the students' material and your own.

Clarify discrepancies, draw attention to contradictory and supportive data, correct misleading interpretations.

Watching for news

Current information is available in newspapers, trade magazines, professional journals, and the electronic media. Designate members to keep track of one medium each and report on items of relevance. Incorporate that information into the ongoing course discussion.

Selecting a textbook

Give a sample chapter from several texts being considered to small evaluation teams, which will report to the whole class on the pros and cons of the text.

You might want to provide them with guidelines for their assessment: reading level appropriate to the group; clarity of explanations; style of writing; quality of illustrations; bibliography; index; plus other criteria suitable to your setting.

Really using a textbook

Assign just a section of a text to be read prior to a given class. Provide written questions that help focus attention on the most important points. Draw attention also to supporting and peripheral

issues. With the basics already covered through the readings, a foundation has been established for further discussions and teacher input. As is to be expected with assigned readings, some people will be better prepared than others. But that is their choice. The advantages of this approach – the sharing of responsibility for learning – tend to outweigh any shortcomings.

CLASSIC CONCEPT

Learning from experience

Give participants every opportunity to transfer insights from experiential learning into their everyday behavior. Kurt Lewin provides the theoretical foundation for a three-phase model.[1] Use it as a planning checklist: the more consideration you give to each, the higher the chances for individual discoveries.

- Phase one: experience the action: the learner experiences an action by trying out a set of behaviors, a strategy or procedure.

- Phase two: observe the consequences: the learner experiences the result of the actions by receiving feedback and through reflection on the experience.

- Phase three: develop an action theory: the learner is prompted to organize the new information into an action theory – a statement that describes what actions are needed to achieve a desired consequence in a given situation. "If I behave in such and such a way, then this and that will happen."

To some, the use of library facilities and data bases is an everyday undertaking; to others it's downright scary. One way to anticipate and build on these differences involves assignments with differing complexity. This allows participants to select a task at their comfort level without having to make a public admission (or a cover-up) of their lack of experience.

The first aims at developing the skills of analysis, summary, and application of relevant data. The second assignment involves familiarization with the tools of library research, including computerized data bases, catalogues, abstracts, and indexes. Participants are handed the following outline.

• *Assignment one: executive summary*

An executive summary recapitulates a body of information and provides a thumbnail synopsis of one or more sources. Your task is to investigate and summarize a topic of special interest to you. The topic must fit into the course agenda and provide valuable information to your classmates.

Your choice of presentation methods will be influenced by the nature of your topic and by the class timetable. Please discuss this with me.

To get you started, here's a list of possible topics.

1. How do seating arrangements influence power structure?

2. What leadership behaviors are most effective in task-oriented groups?

3. Summarize the essentials of Robert's Rules of Order and identify their pros and cons.

4. Select two or three publications from our list and search and summarize recent articles on small-group behavior.

• *Assignment two: annotated bibliography*

This type of bibliography identifies publications pertaining to our topic. In your annotation give a two- or three-sentence summary and critical evaluation of the content. Ideally, an annotated bibliography gives the reader a quick overview of what's available; gives details on title, author, publisher, and date; and provides a succinct content summary.

Several people have agreed to prepare bibliographies on related topics. Please complete yours by (date) so that we can collate them into one document.

Please use the following format.

William Strunk, Jr. (and E.B. White, editor). The elements of style. *New York: Macmillan, 1972. (78 pages)*

A classic distinguished by brevity, clarity, and good sense. The most concise book on the fundamentals of composition.

Peter Elbow. Writing with power. *New York: Oxford University Press, 1981. (384 pages)*

A practical handbook with down-to-earth advice for beginning and seasoned writers. Not about getting power over the reader, but over yourself and the writing process. (Includes a twelve-item bibliography on publishing, and an index.)

Henriette Klauser. Writing on both sides of the brain. *San Francisco: Harper Row, 1986. (139 pages)*

How to use right-brain techniques to release your expressive powers. Good stuff on ordering ideas, overcoming procrastination, whole-brain spelling, and using visualization for creative purposes. Good ideas on overcoming writer's block while staring at your word-processor monitor.

Show articles in journals and chapters from edited collections as follows.

Jules Henri Poincare. "Mathematical creation," in The creative process, *ed. Brewster Ghiselin. New York: New American Library, 1952, p.38.*

21 Writing in journals

The object of reflection is invariably the discovery of something satisfying to the mind which was not there at the beginning of the search.

– Ernest Dimnet (1866-1954), French priest, lecturer, and author.

Learning journals, also called logs or diaries, are simple tools that can help to integrate learning from inside and outside the classroom. They further create a confidential connection between teacher and learner, or among small groups of participants. They are also excellent tools for teaching the skills of observing and reflecting.

Journals are best used to ...
- assist participants in making connections between course material and personal lives and work
- draw participants' attention to personal learning opportunities that might otherwise be overlooked
- provide participants with a structure to keep track of multiple experiences during a course or workshop
- collect material that can be used during debriefing and evaluation sessions

Group size

Since this is an individual exercise, the size of the participant group puts no limitation on this tool. However, the optional sharing of the information requires the intimacy of small groups.

Time required

Most of the recording is done on the participants' own time. But it can be very useful, especially with novice diarists, to dedicate five-minute periods during class time for individual entries.

Materials needed

Ask participants to set aside either a small notebook or a section of their binder. Unless people explicitly wish to make their journal entries public, confidentiality must be guaranteed.

How to proceed

1. Introduce the idea.
Explain how a journal permits the recording of personal impressions, experiences, and questions over a given time span. Even a one-day workshop can yield much valuable data which, if unrecorded, would be lost to conscious memory.

If you plan to use a journal in conjunction with classroom activities, explain how easily we can become overwhelmed with information and miss out on meaningful connections and applications. A journal provides a possible remedy.

If the journal is to be used in conjunction with field work, internships, or independent learning projects, phrase the explanation accordingly. See the sidebar for innovative uses of journals.

2. Emphasize privacy.
Underscore the private nature of these entries, but add that you would appreciate it if people would share their entries with the class, particular individuals, or yourself, either at certain times during the course or at the end.

3. Explain the process.
Give an example of what might go into the journal and how to record events. Offer examples, verbally or in written form. (See the written sample provided below.)

Find out who has had previous practice with educational journals and invite old hands to briefly describe their experience. Be prepared to balance such descriptions. You might ask everyone to suspend their judgment for a while.

4. Provide a structure for systematic recording.
At certain points of the course allow time for participants to pause, reflect, and record. With inexperienced journal-keepers, provide key questions to guide them through the exercise.

5. Arrange for ways to exchange information (optional).
Invite individuals to share whatever they wish, either with a partner or in small groups of not more than three. Sharing selected data does several things: it reduces isolation, validates individual experiences, and provides new ways of viewing common experiences. Following the small-group sessions, issues of interest to the whole class could be aired – with confidentiality preserved by such preambles as "Our group raised the concern that ..." or "We were surprised to discover that...."

By arrangement, you may ask to read each journal at regular intervals. This will give you the opportunity to gain insights and feedback you

Experience seems to be like the shining of a bright lantern. It suddenly makes clear in the mind what was already there, perhaps, but dim.

– Walter de la Mare (1873-1956), English poet and novelist.

wouldn't otherwise have access to. You are also given an opportunity to respond to individual concerns on a one-to-one basis. If the situation seems appropriate, you can later raise important issues in class while still honoring individual confidentiality.

6. Suggest ways of writing

As your group becomes more and more experienced with journal-writing, you can offer directions and suggest certain themes and topics to focus on. This still leaves room for unstructured, personal commentaries.

For short-term courses or special projects, journals can be used on a one-time basis only. Of the examples provided on the next pages, **A** asks the student to reflect on the emotions surrounding plans for a job placement. Examples **B** and **C** require more complex reflections: first on individual behavior, then on a group process, and finally on possible action.

Maintaining a journal during a field project

Students on work assignments benefit from regular communication with their instructor. Both parties need to monitor how things are working out. Where face-to-face meetings are difficult to arrange, a written log or journal may be the answer.

From the outset, the student must be encouraged to express any concern or question – about the placement, the on-site sponsor, the relevance of assignments, or any other matter. Assure participants that no one but the instructor will read the entries without their permission. You'll be astonished at how honest students can be.

For best results, provide learners with a recording system. It supports self-exploration and helps to develop observation and reporting skills. In the example

below, the students had discussed the giving and receiving of feedback and participated in a role-play about feedback. Their log for the following two weeks asked them to observe and describe performance-related comments directed at them.

The following questions are designed to stimulate recall and focus reflection.

- How did you do in your placement today? Please provide a brief description of the tasks, the site, and the people you worked with.

- How do you feel about this latest work assignment?

- If you received any feedback about your work, address the following questions. Who gave the feedback? What were the circumstances? How did you feel at the time? What did you say/do upon receiving feedback? Illustrate your answers with specific examples.

- Describe what you would do differently the next time you receive feedback on your performance.

- If you had occasion to provide feedback to another person, describe the circumstances: what did you say, to whom, about what? Describe the other person's reaction. How did you feel when all was said and done?

- Describe what you have learned about receiving and giving feedback. Be as specific as you can.

- Describe what you would do differently the next time you offer feedback to a coworker.

Example A

Date:_____ Topic:_____

What happened:

> Today Peter mentioned that we were required to visit a hotel and arrange for a four-hour practicum. We are supposed to do it at a place where we would like to work some day. He said he wouldn't make the arrangements for us, but gave us a letter of introduction. The rest is up to each of us.

How I feel/felt about it:

> I am not sure if I like this: going to a strange place to ask such a favour makes me nervous. What if they are too busy? What sort of place would I like to visit? Maybe this would be a good exercise for me to see if I really like the hotel business. Peter says that the people are usually very friendly.

Action plan:

> I will look at the list of hotels Peter gave us and pick two that appeal to me. I'll go to each sometime before the next class, just to have a look around. From these impressions, I'll pick the place I like best. Then I might be ready to make that phone call.

With headings provided by the instructor

We ... write to heighten our own awareness of life.... We write to taste life twice, in the moment and in retrospection.... When I don't write I feel my world shrinking. I feel I lose my fire, my color.

– Anaïs Nin, *The Diary of Anaïs Nin*, volume V.

Example B

Completing the Learning Loop

Date: _____ Topic: _____

1. What questions do you have as a result of todays' learning experience? Jot down two or three.

2. From these questions, what key concepts can you extract? List at least two for each question.

3. How can you go about finding answers to these questions? For each question, select at least one specific approach you can take.

Example C

Evaluating - Reflecting - Planning

Date: _____ My role:_____

I learned these three things about the way task groups operate.
- _____
- _____
- _____

If I were to assess my own behavior during the task, I'd say that ...
_____
_____
_____

If I could make one change about my participation in the group, I would ...
_____
_____
_____

If I do change my behavior, here's how I'll know that I have been successful.
_____
_____
_____

So the point of my keeping a notebook has never been, nor is it now, to have an accurate factual record of what I have been doing or thinking.... How it felt to me: that is getting closer to the truth about a notebook.

– Joan Didion, "On Keeping a Notebook."

Three case studies

Case #1: Chronicling a placement experience

At Boston College, undergraduates were assigned one of thirty-five different placements, from tutoring refugees to working in a residential setting with abused children.[1] For many students, this was their first serious challenge of previously established opinions, values, and priorities. Their course work asked them to examine the failures of institutions and the effect these have on the lives of individuals. By using journals, students found an outlet for troubling questions and their own feelings. Their instructor stressed the need to be sensitive to the confidential nature of journal entries. But once a level of trust had been established she was able to use the journal materials (anonymously) during class discussions and suggest alternate ways of viewing the problems confronting the students.

Case #2: Recording experiences thematically

In the community involvement program at Macalester College, St. Paul, Minnesota, students were encouraged to organize journals thematically in a loose-leaf binder.[2] Some themes reflected the writer's personal life (such as dreams, fears, and relationships); others addressed aspects of relationships with institutions, their current job, or the educational program. Within each theme, students were encouraged to create subcategories pertaining to work, practicum, or academic life. "Be ritualistic," their instructor recommended. "Set aside a time every day for reflection and writing. Be analytical. Allot 20 percent of writing time for describing the problem and 80 for possible solutions. Be optimistic. Even a placement that falls apart offers a rich source of learning."

Case #3: Journals as professional conversations

At McGill University in Montreal, two-way journals are used to document an ongoing dialogue between mentor and trainee during professional training in education, dietetics, and nursing.[3] The writing is used deliberately as an instructional device, in which instructors, as expert practitioners, give direction and feedback to interns. This professional conversation provides opportunities for trainees to raise questions regarding their placement. In their written responses, "instructors assist the integration of learning and the framing of mechanisms for deriving meaning from the practicum experience and theory and skill classes."

Students are told about the importance of intentional reflection and the merits of writing as part of their professional development. They are assured that this kind of writing is neither academic nor objective, and are encouraged to express their emotional responses. Such personal writing serves, among other purposes, to vent "problems, frustrations and high points of the day." They are told to record their reflections frequently and as soon as possible after the event. Using loose-leaf binders allows the instructor to read and respond, while the learner continues to write the journal on pages that can be inserted when the binder is returned. For the most positive response, journals are made a practicum requirement, but are not graded in any way.

With large classes and intensive schedules, students and instructors benefit from this written conversation. Students have private access to their teacher and can set the agenda for that encounter. Instructors learn more about each learner, can stimulate thinking through probing questions, and receive valuable feedback on the placement experience. Most importantly, "these professional conversations provide learners with explicit modeling of the productive use of reflecting; they have a window on the reflection and decision-making processes of the expert practitioner."

22

Assessing the course

We learn by trial and error, not by trial and rightness. If we did things correctly every time, we would never have to change directions – we'd just continue the current course and end up with more of the same.

– Roger von Oech, *A Whack on the Side of the Head.*

There are many ways to gauge the success of a course. Customarily, some sort of standard evaluation form is handed out near the end, asking, among other things, that participants "rate the refreshment service on a scale of 1 to 5." Such indexes hardly yield information of value to course designer and teacher. Another problem with routine evaluations is their timing; you won't get thoughtful responses amid the rush of end-of-course activities.

Choose your timing carefully

To obtain meaningful opinions and suggestions, set time aside and make this a legitimate course component. Asking for feedback after the first day, a major activity, halfway through, or just before the end will bring interesting information to light and permit corrective action before it's too late.

Explain the importance of feedback

Tell participants why you are asking and what you plan to do with the information. Solicit their careful attention and invite candid responses. Share the collected information with the group and process it. In a multi-session course, I have asked for written feedback on Day One and brought the comments – summarized on newsprint – back to start Day Two. This took only about twenty minutes, but demonstrated how much I valued the input and made it obvious that I was prepared to respond to the issues.

Give it a fresh name

Instead of calling this an evaluation – which suggests judging or grading – think of less loaded labels for this activity. Feedback, check-up, taking stock, feeling the pulse, assessment, opinionnaire, or inventory might do.

Invite participants to design the evaluation

Whenever possible, involve participants in the design of the feedback process. If a form is to be used, ask for help in its design. To make best use of class time, you could start with a collection of forms and ask groups to contribute questions that should be on them. Make sure your own questions are added as well. If you have the time and if the atmosphere is right for it, invite groups to come up with creative ways of giving feedback; they may end up using collages, slide shows, "award" ceremonies, skits, or scrapbooks as very effective feedback mechanisms.

Keep good records

In addition to the participants' comments, record your personal remarks about the group, the course, the ups and downs. When the time comes for a repeat performance, you can make good use of these notes in your planning. Let them also be a measure of your own development: you'll notice you are getting better!

Examples

Here are a few forms to get you started. Use them as they are or change them to suit your needs. Strive for a balance of questions to bring out critical as well as supportive comments.

If it's worth teaching, it's worth finding out whether the instruction was successful. If it wasn't entirely successful, it's worth finding out how to improve it.

– Robert Mager, Making Instruction Work.

Daily Questionnaire

What do you consider today's most valuable experience?

Why is that?

What aspect of today's activities could have been strengthened ?

How could that be done?

What other comments do you have?

Your name _____

optional

This is the most versatile of all. It can be filled out at various stages of the course. It concentrates on high and low points and asks the respondent to give reasons for each issue.

Our First Session Together
Please finish the sentences below.

When I first walked into the room ...

Now that the session is over I wish ...

My first impression of the instructor was ...

The get-acquainted activity was ...

I found the small-group activities ...

About the proposed course outline I think ...

I'd also like you to know that ...

The first session together in a new group can be overwhelming for many participants. This form asks them to look back, report their feelings and impressions, and identify the highlights. Teachers can use the same form. Follow-up discussions can bring information to light that would otherwise be missed.

CLASSIC CONCEPT

Domains of learning

Robert Gagné holds that learning is not one process, but consists of domains, depending on what is to be learned.[1] When planning educational activities, be aware of the domain you are dealing with.

- *The cognitive domain deals with the recall or recognition of knowledge and the development of intellectual abilities and skills.*

- *The affective domain describes changes in attitude and values, and the development of appreciations and adequate adjustment.*

- *The psychomotor domain has to do with the development of manipulative skills, involving tools, machinery, procedures, and techniques.*

Halfway Through

We are at the halfway mark of your workshop and this seems a good point to stop and see how we are doing. I am particularly interested in your views of the way each session is structured, my own performance, and your sense of the usefulness of it all.

Please complete the following sentences.

1. The structure of the sessions ...

_____

_____

and I wish we ...

_____

_____

2. About your performance, I'd like to say that ...

_____

_____

and I wish you ...

_____

_____

3. I wish we did more ...

_____

_____

4. I wish we did less ...

_____

_____

5. With only three more sessions remaining, I suggest we ...

_____

_____

6. To sum up my feelings about the workshop, I'd say ...

_____

_____

_____
signed

This is another variation using the unfinished sentence technique to obtain quite personal information about the course and its direction.

Self-Evaluation Checklist

	hardly	on and off	quite a lot
I was interested in this unit	☐	☐	☐

What helped or hindered?

_____

I learned about group process	☐	☐	☐

Mostly about

_____

I participated	☐	☐	☐

How

_____

I contributed task functions	☐	☐	☐

Which

_____

I helped build group spirit	☐	☐	☐

How _____

Based on this brief assessment, I have these three goals for the remainder of the course.

1._____
_____.

2._____
_____.

3._____
_____.

This questionnaire was developed for a training event on group leadership and participation skills. Respondents were asked to rate themselves on the quality of their interaction with others. The collected data was discussed with the group. It brought out some common difficulties pertaining to course content and was used to redesign parts of the theory session that followed. Since this form was used with a group of coworkers, a symbol was used for identification to encourage candid responses. Participants quite naturally "owned" their comments during the ensuing discussion. Subsequent forms asked for names instead of codes.

Though not always called upon to condemn ourselves, it is always safe to suspect ourselves.

– Richard Whateley (1787-1863), English logician, Bishop of Dublin.

After the Discussion

Please respond to these questions and be prepared to share your observations during the 4 o'clock debriefing session.

What role(s) did you assume most of the time. Name one or two.

Comment on the effect your contribution might have had on the group's progress.

What is your personal reaction to the way your group worked together?

What problems did you observe in your small group?

What could the instructor do to alleviate the problems you have observed?

What could you do to increase productivity?

What could you do to help build cohesiveness?

_____
                                        signed

He who knows does not speak.
He who speaks does not know.

– Lao Tzu, *Tao Te Ching.*

This questionnaire was designed to assess a section of a workshop on group dynamics. Participants were asked to do two things: reflect on their contribution to the group task and comment on the course design. The form worked because of the mutual respect between learners and facilitator.

23

Giving and receiving feedback

In his commendations I am fed;
It is a banquet to me.

– William Shakespeare,
   Macbeth, Act I, Scene 4.

Personal feedback gives information about behavior, performance, and conduct. If done well, feedback helps participants recognize potential problems and correct them. It can improve performance and interpersonal communications. Occasions to exchange feedback arise frequently in a learning group; following are some examples.

- When you ask small groups to report. Example: "How did you do as a group?"

- When you ask for comments on the progress of the course. Example: "Tell me, how do you like the way we are spending class time?"

- When students comment on teacher behavior. Example: "Your instructions confused me and there was no time to ask for clarification."

- When participants speak to each other. Example: "Kiran, when you got up and started to write things on the flip chart, it really helped us to get focused."

- When you comment on a particular group behavior. Example: "I'm impressed with the quality of work the groups are producing."

- When you offer feedback to an individual after a specific behavior. Examples: "Thank you Sandy, for bringing us back to the agenda – the discussion was drifting off topic" or "Evan, you have answered almost every question I have posed: could you sit back for a little while and let others have a go?"

Guidelines

Here are some guidelines that make the process simple and educational. They address both the giving and the receiving of feedback information.

- **Give and receive with care.**

Above all else, giving and receiving feedback is an act of caring. It is an exchange of gifts. Ideally, the sender's intentions are simple: Please listen to what I've noticed about you. You may find it useful information, or you may not. It's just my perception and you don't have to do anything about it.

The receiver, to make best use of the feedback, accepts it: Thank you for taking the trouble to share your observations and to share them with me. I'll take what you tell me as information, as your view of my behavior. I may or may not agree with you and I am under no obligation to behave differently.

- **Ask to be invited.**

Most people are more receptive to potentially sensitive information if they have either requested it ("Tell me what you saw me do") or when someone has first asked them ("May I give you some feedback about ...?").

- **Concentrate on behavior.**

Behavioral feedback is about what can be observed, not about hunches, inferences, second-guesses, or judgments. Example: "You are very quiet tonight," instead of "You aren't interested in what we are doing?"

- **Make it easy to receive.**

Describe the behavior on a continuum of "more or less," rather than as "either/or." Example: "Daily journal entries are a good idea; your writing has become much more detailed since you began four weeks ago," instead of "We are half-way through the course and your entries are still without focus."

- **Don't delay.**

Feedback carries more weight if given soon after the observation. The person can then relate it to the specific situation and internalize the information more meaningfully.

- **Small doses, please.**

Give just enough information for the other to digest. Overloading someone with information dramatically reduces the effect. Dumping large amounts of information may give instant relief to the sender, but it makes it very difficult for the receiver to process.

- **Feedback comes in different disguises.**

Feedback doesn't always come in the spoken form. It can be communicated through gestures, eye contact, body stance, and relative distance to others. However, these messages may be misinterpreted. Quite often, nonverbal messages make a stronger impact than spoken ones. Ensure that your expression and body language is congruent with your verbal message.

Do not search for the truth; only cease to cherish opinions.

– Sengtsan, *hsin hsin ming*. Sengtsan (?-606) spent his life as a wandering Buddhist monk. The title's first character Hsin shows a man standing by [his?] words, and is often translated as faith or trust. The second Hsin depicts the heart, and has come to mean heart, mind, soul.

How to better hear the feedback you are given

1. Concentrate on listening.

You don't need to do anything with the feedback. Simply look at the person giving you the feedback and listen carefully. Try to hear the words, see the gestures, and remember to keep breathing.

There is a story of Buddha, sitting under a tree, meditating. A man approaches him, full of rage. Buddha looks at the anger as a gift, but instead of taking it as expected, he thanks the man and regrets that he won't be able to accept his present.

2. Don't feel you have to respond immediately.

Most of us have difficulty hearing both positive and negative things about ourselves. To cover our discomfort, we guard ourselves with quick responses. Unfortunately, valuable opportunities for growth are lost and both sender and receiver lose out. The receiver is prevented from hearing the full message and the sender may think twice before offering feedback again. Avoid the following defenses.

- diverting: "I think that most people ..."

- explaining: "That's because ..."

- rejecting: "Yes, but ..."

- discounting: "Gee, that wasn't anything special ..."

- intellectualizing: "From a post-structuralist viewpoint ..."

- attacking: "Who are you to make such comments ..."

- whining: "If only I had advance warning, I'd ..."

3. Make sure you understand.

However much both parties may try, not every feedback message arrives neatly packaged and clearly understood. Giving and receiving involves a conscious effort on the part of both people involved. If you don't understand, say so, but let the other person know which part of the feedback message is unclear to you ("You are saying that my contributions irritate you. But I'm not sure how. Could you give me an example?"). Now both are engaged in working towards an understanding of the issue.

Occasionally, a third person – the teacher or another participant – may step in to ask for clarification ("Did I miss something here? I don't think you heard what that group is asking for."). The thing to do now is check with the parties involved and find out how satisfied they are with the exchange.

4. Say when enough is enough.

Should people get carried away and end up overwhelming someone with suggestions, advice, or criticism, it is the recipient's prerogative to say so. If things seem to be getting out of hand, the teacher must intervene ("Sean, that may be enough feedback for you right now – what do you say?").

How to confront a difficult behavior

Every so often, people behave in ways that irritate and interfere. Confronting this calls for a clear focus on behavior – not the person. Joseph Raelin offers a three-part memory aid, known as "when/I/because."[1]

- **Part one:** The "when" is followed by the naming of the specific behavior. For example: "When you read your newspaper during the group discussion...." Note that the behavior is described objectively and that no blame or value judgement is attached.

- **Part two:** The "I" statement follows with a description of the feeling you experience as a result of the behavior. "When you read your newspaper during the group discussion, I felt let down." Note how the feedback provider is taking ownership for the feeling, rather than holding the other responsible. Citing feelings in this manner personalizes the feedback and adds meaning to the exchange.

- **Part three:** The "because" part of the statement informs the recipient of the effect of the behavior. "When you read your newspaper during the group discussion, I felt let down because you didn't share any of your expertise. Also, by tuning out you made the task more difficult for your group." Hearing the consequences stated in a clear manner will make it easier for the recipient to listen and respond nondefensively. The path is paved for both partners to engage in problem-solving.

24

Designing tests and quizzes

Which do you consider were the most alike, Caesar or Pompeii, or vice versa? (Be brief.)

– This and the following test questions appear in *1066 And All That*, a satire upon textbook history and our confused recollection of it.

In his autobiography, Malcolm Knowles ranks "learning about meaningful evaluation" as one of the eight episodes that changed his life.[1] On the road to this discovery, he had to shed the belief that evaluation had to be quantitative, limited to the type of pencil-and-paper tests most of us know and dread. He learned to use many of the qualitative approaches mentioned in these pages, including interviewing, observer feedback, journals, case studies, and self-assessments.

Meaningful evaluation helps participants gain insights into how and what they are learning. According to Stephen Brookfield, "the only educational justification for evaluation is to assist learning."[2] Therefore, evaluation activities must be integrated into every learning activity, regardless of whether the course intent is the acquisition of information, the development of skills, or the exploration of feelings and attitudes.

More than before-and-after testing

Written tests still have a place, but they must be used in a new way. In the traditional scenario, an instructor might begin the day with these remarks: "Before starting the course, please complete the pretest so that we know your entry knowledge. It'll help us assess your progress later." At the end of the day, participants complete another test that attempts to measure their progress and "satisfy the course requirements."[3]

By contrast, in a course that integrates evaluation with other learning activities, the day starts out differently: "Let's begin with a self-assessment of your knowledge, skills, and attitudes. This will help you think about the work that lies ahead." At the end of the course, a concluding test is introduced in a similar light: "As I mentioned this morning and throughout the day, our last activity is another self-assessment. It'll help you to review what we have covered and identify what you've learned." Finally, participants are reminded that they'll be contacted again in the near future for a similar test – this one to reinforce what's been learned and to determine how useful the new learning is.

Note that the evaluation design still uses written tests, but it is now solidly based on these adult learning principles: learning is amplified if participants know what they will learn; it is further enhanced by immediate reinforcement (through the end-of-day test) and over the long term (through the follow-up survey).[4]

Benefits of written tests

Learners and teacher benefit from carefully thought-out evaluation activities.

To the learner they provide ...
- realistic short-term goals
- motivation to study notes, texts, and handouts
- increased retention of learned material
- direct feedback on progress
- objective evidence of accomplishment

Teachers and course planners derive ...
- ways to assess the appropriateness of instructional objectives
- evaluation of teaching techniques and materials
- feedback on teaching effectiveness
- support and reward for everyone's efforts

Ideally, tests should reflect clearly defined instructional objectives. Techniques of writing instructional objectives and designing tests are beyond the scope of this book, but the following summaries and checklists will prepare you for further exploration.[5]

Types of tests

The tests with everyday application are called objective tests, since the correct answer can be objectively determined. *Selection-type* tests require the learner to choose one or more of the given responses; examples include multiple-choice, true-false, and matching-items types. *Supply-type* tests ask the learner to provide a correct response; examples include short-answer and essay questions.

- • **Multiple-choice items**

Each starts with a *stem* and is followed by four or five *alternatives*. Example:

> Which province lies between Alaska and Washington?
> a. Alberta
> <u>b</u>. British Columbia
> c. Yukon
> d. Oregon

Estimate the size of
(1) Little Arthur.
(2) Friar Puck.
(3) Magna Charta.

Experienced test designers follow certain ground rules in the construction of multiple-choice tests.[6] Use this checklist to see how well your test items measure up.

☐ Each item measures only important learning outcome.

☐ The stem is stated in simple, clear language.

☐ Most of the wording is in the stem, rather than the alternatives.

☐ The stem is stated in positive form, wherever possible.

☐ Negative wording is emphasized whenever it is used in the stem.

☐ The intended answer is correct or clearly best.

☐ All alternatives are grammatically consistent with the stem.

☐ The item contains no verbal clues to enable learners to select the correct answer or to eliminate an incorrect alternative.

☐ The length of correct answers is varied to eliminate length as a clue.

☐ "All of the above" is not used as an alternative.

☐ "None of the above" is used with extreme caution.

☐ The position of the correct answer is varied in random order.

☐ Each item is independent of other items in the test.

Have you the faintest recollection of
(1) Ethelbreth?
(2) Athelthral?
(3) Thruthelthrolth?

• **True-false items**

Here the learner is required to judge a declarative statement as either true or false. Alternatives to true-false may be yes/no, agree/disagree, right/wrong, fact/opinion, and the like. Examples:

<u>True</u> False	The rivers Mosel and Rhein join near the city of Koblenz.
<u>Agree</u> Disagree	The kestrel is also known as the sparrow hawk.
Fact <u>Opinion</u>	White wine should be drunk with seafood.

You can also combine multiple-choice and true-false items.

Grape varieties permitted under Bordeaux Appellation Contrôlée rules include:

A. Pinot Noir   T <u>F</u>

B. Cabernet Franc   <u>T</u> F

C. Chardonnay   T <u>F</u>

D. Merlot   <u>T</u> F

E. Semillon   <u>T</u> F

In addition, learners may be asked to judge the statement as true or false, and then provide a true statement. They may be further asked to explain their choice in a short statement. The problem with true-false items is that they are very difficult to construct; they must be either undeniably true or clearly false. There is also a danger of discrimination against learners capable of perceiving possible exceptions to even the most obvious true or false answer.

Use this checklist to help keep each of your true-false items honest.[7]

☐ The statement includes only one central significant idea.

☐ The statement is worded as unquestioningly true or false.

☐ The statement is short and uses a simple language structure.

☐ The statement contains no double negatives.

☐ Statement of opinions are attributed to a source.

☐ Overall, negative statements are used sparingly.

Estimate the average age of
(1) The Ancient Britons.
(2) Ealdormen.
(3) Old King Cole.

- **Matching items**

The matching item is a modification of the multiple-choice format, consisting of two lists – a series of stems, called *premises*, and several *responses*. For instance, lists may contain parts of a diagram and names of the parts, problems and solutions, countries and capitals. The learner must match the items on one list with those on the other. Here is an example from an equestrian test.

Directions: Column A contains a list of basic tack; Column B a list of variation on basic tack. On the line at the left of each tack item, put the letter of the item in Column B that best fits the item. Each response in Column B may be used once, more than once, or not at all.

Column A	Column B
(D) 1. Bridle	A. Bridoon
(E) 2. Saddle	B. Chin harness
(C) 3. Rein	C. Martingale
(A) 4. Double bridle	D. Snaffle
	E. Sweat flap

In a matching-items test, all responses must appear as plausible alternatives for each premise. If that is not possible, resort to separate multiple-choice items.

- **Short-answer items**

  These consist of a question or an incomplete statement to which the learner is asked to supply a response. Among the many variations, three are most straightforward: direct question, fill-in-the blank, and association.

  Direct question:

  In what part of North America does the ruby-throated hummingbird live? _____ *(the East)*

  Fill-in-the-blank:

  Unlike most birds, cardinals mate for _____. *(life)*

  Association or identification:

  After each (male) bird listed below, write the dominant color.

  1. Baltimore oriole   _____ *(orange)*
  2. Steller's jay   _____ *(blue)*
  3. Northern cardinal   _____ *(red)*
  4. Northern mockingbird   _____ *(gray)*

  Let this checklist help you construct and evaluate short-answer items.[8]

  ☐ The length of the statement is kept uniformly short.

  ☐ For each statement, only a single, brief answer is possible.

  ☐ The blank is at the end of the statement.

  ☐ The learner is not required to supply such words as "the" and "an."

- **Essay question**

  This test item consists of a question, topic, or brief statement to which the learner must supply an extended response. According to one authority, essay questions have many uses, including the measurement of a person's ability to make comparisons, apply principles, organize and summarize information, communicate ideas, conduct a critical study, make judgments, draw inferences, be persuasive, use logical reasoning, and demonstrate in-depth knowledge of a topic.[9] The following are examples of essay-type questions.

  - Describe the principles of ... (summarizing)
  - What additional data are needed to ... (inferring)
  - Propose a solution ... (creating)

  To the teacher, essay questions offer the advantage of quick construction and the disadvantage of the time it takes to evaluate each. Subjectivity in scoring presents a further complication. In fact, some

Which came first, A.D. or B.C.? (Be careful.)

studies report that independent grading of the same essay by several teachers can result in marks from excellent to failing and that the same teachers grading the same essay at different times gave significantly different grades.[10] The quality of handwriting and composition can also have a negative influence on the one who grades.

Whether you have to assign a grade or are free to do without them, your learners are entitled to careful comments. To that end, evaluation should always be *educative*. That is, feedback should assist learners in three ways: to become more adept and critically reflective about the task; to gain insights into their habitual learning processes and enable them to decide whether to maintain or alter them; and to nurture their self-confidence as learners.[11] Aim for these goals every time you evaluate an essay question. Instead of a cursory check mark for a right answer, or a routine "well done!", say what you find good about the essay, assess how the learner has demonstrated (or failed to show) proficiency in the material under study, acknowledge any progress from previous work, and indicate areas for further growth.

This last checklist will assist you in writing and scoring essay questions.[12]

Preparation
☐ Participants have had prior practice (not graded) in understanding and responding to essay questions.
☐ The participants are clear on the scoring method and know to what extent organization of the material, handwriting, grammar, etc. are taken into account.

Test design
☐ The directions are specific and to the point. The learner knows exactly what's expected.
☐ The vocabulary and jargon are consistent with the learner's experience.
☐ The time it takes to answer each essay question is about twice as long as it takes the teacher to write the answer. (Adjust this, depending on participants' familiarity with the subject matter and the process of testing.)
☐ The test contains more than one essay question and offers a choice of questions to be answered. This increases participants' chances to be successful.
☐ The value for each question (or part thereof) is given on the test paper.

Evaluation
☐ Learners' names are concealed or coded to reduce personal biases.
☐ Questions are evaluated one at a time, on all tests. This tends to increase reliability in scoring.
☐ Each learner receives personalized comments in line with the goals outlined above.

Write not more than two lines on The Career of Napoleon Buonaparte, or The Acquisition of our Indian Empire, or The Prime Ministers of England.
N.B. Do not on any account attempt to write on both sides of the paper at once.

25

Projecting overhead

*A picture is worth
a thousand words.*

– Anonymous

Next to a chalk or white board, the overhead projector is the most widely available visual device. You can make transparencies quite easily, either by writing and drawing directly onto the acetate or with transfers, using an ordinary duplicating machine. This chapter provides some straightforward instruction on how to make transparencies, how to operate the machine, and where to place it in a room.

Advantages of the overhead projector

- The machine can be operated from the front of the room while the presenter faces the audience.

- The time spent on each item is completely under the presenter's control. The lamp can be switched on or off to project the image at certain times. A transparency can be brought back at a later time for review and to stimulate recall and discussion.

- Room lights remain on, so that learners can take notes.

- Since the transparencies are right-side-up as you look over the projector, you rarely need to lose eye contact with your audience.

- Instead of individual transparency sheets, you can use a roll of transparency sheeting, making the machine into a continuous bulletin board. If needed, you can wind back to review previous writing. Later, the roll can either be stored for review or cleaned for reuse.

- The sequence of a presentation is easily modified by the deletion or insertion of transparencies.

How to prepare transparencies

You can write directly on transparency sheets or use a duplicating machine to transfer an image from a sheet of paper onto a transparency. With the direct method, use special marking pens; they are available in many colors, some water-based (erasable) others alcohol-based (permanent). With the machine method, use a clean original and copy in either black and white or full color. If you have access to cardboard frames, mount the transparency and use the frame to record your notes and reminders.

Basic transparency design

1. Check the size.

The usable surface of a standard transparency frame is 7-1/2" x 9-1/2", so your prepared copy must not exceed these dimensions. If you omit the cardboard frame, your usable light surface becomes 8" x 10" in size.

2. Keep it simple.

Too much detail creates confusion; after all, the image is meant to support your verbal presentation, not take its place.

Use no more than six words per line and six or fewer lines per image. Select only key words and phrases. Don't try to summarize an entire presentation on one transparency.

3. Apply layout rules.

Double-space all lines. Use simple, bold lettering types, at least 1/4" high. Plain type is best. Horizontal is considered the best format, although vertical is acceptable.

4. Avoid typewritten material.

It does not project well, even if it is large type. Some laser printers may do a better job, as long as you follow this rule: if you can read the original at a distance of ten feet, the transparency should project well.

5. Make transparencies into handouts.

Transparencies can be photocopied and become handout material for people who missed a session.

6. Special effects.

Unusual effects, such as silhouettes and cutouts, are easily prepared. Two superimposition methods are possible: one involves stacking transparencies layer upon layer, thus illustrating complex models and processes as you talk about them. The other method involves projecting an image onto a writing surface, such as a white board, and adding the details by writing on that surface.

Operational dos and don'ts

- DON'T show more information than is necessary at one time. If you show too much, viewers will get ahead of you or their minds will wander; either way, they won't pay attention to you.

- DO use the revelation technique. Place a sheet of heavy paper under the transparency. By moving the sheet down, you reveal the image line-by-line and thus control the viewers' attention.

- DON'T turn the lamp on before you have positioned a transparency. The bright white field on the screen is annoying to look at – yet everyone will.

- DO line up the image and when it's needed, turn on the lamp. When it is no longer needed, turn the lamp off. Switch whenever you want to tear your audience away from the lit image. You may be talking about a new bit of information, but if the old transparency is still on, you can count on people still looking at it. Light fascinates.

- DON'T turn off the room lights. At most, turn down the lights immediately over the projector. Otherwise, natural and electric lights can stay on to allow note-taking and minimize disruption of the proceedings.

- DO use overlays to provide a sense of progression. Up to four transparencies can be placed upon each other in succession with the light shining through. This is particularly effective for flow charts, graphs, and complex models. Start with a simple image, and as you describe additional features, build it up one sheet at a time.

- DON'T wave your hands or other objects over the transparency. The shadow, multiplied many times, will show on the screen and become another irritation.

- DO indicate an item on the transparency by placing a pencil or other pointed object that won't roll away. Like an arrow, it'll focus viewers' attention. Remember to remove the pointer when it has served its purpose.

Room setup

You'll rarely have the ideal physical setting, so check the room beforehand and arrange the furniture to suit your needs. The following diagrams illustrate some setup possibilities, but you'll have to improvise on the spot.

This could be any classroom. Sometimes the screen is mounted so that it sits in the middle of the front wall, right behind the presenter's desk, often obscuring the chalk board when pulled down.

But don't let that deter you. Come early, inspect the setup and see if you can get a portable screen and put it off to the side. Following are a few ideas for good arrangements.

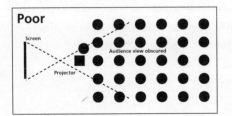

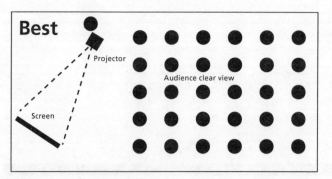

When using an overhead projector, arrange the room so that the audience's view of the screen is not obstructed.

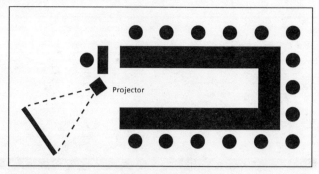

U-table arrangement. *Suitable for thirty people or fewer. This arrangement is ideal for group discussion and interaction.*

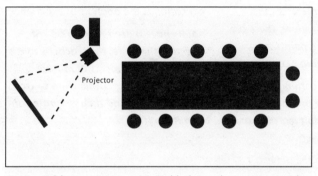

Centre table arrangement. *Suitable for under twenty people. This setup promotes discussion and is best for long meetings.*

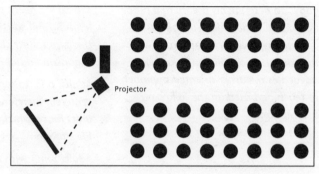

Auditorium/theater arrangement. *(Single projector) Suitable for any size audience, but most efficient for large groups.*

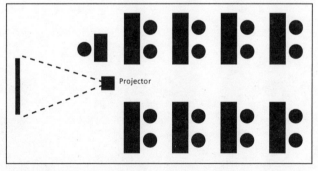

Classroom arrangement. *This is a standard arrangement suitable for any size group.*

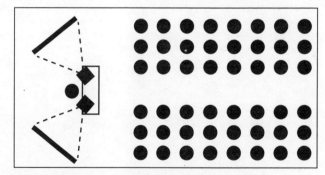

Auditorium/theater arrangement. *(Dual projectors) As above, this arrangement works well with large groups. Two projectors and screens give the presenter more latitude in her or his presentation.*

These diagrams were provided by the 3M Company

The practice of andragogy

Malcolm Knowles uses the term "andragogy" to describe his theory and practice of adult education (in contrast to "pedagogy," which is concerned with the education of children).[1] Knowles advocates a learner-oriented approach to teaching based on the following assumptions.

- Adults are motivated to learn as they experience needs and interests that learning will satisfy; therefore, these are the appropriate starting points for organizing adult learning activities.

- Adults' orientation to learning is life-centered; therefore, the appropriate units for organizing adult learning are life situations, not subjects.

- Adults bring with them the richest resource for their own learning; therefore, the core methodology of adult education is the analysis of experience.

- Adults have a deep need to be self-directed; therefore, the teacher's role is to engage in a process of mutual inquiry with them rather than to transmit knowledge and then evaluate conformity to it.

26   *Flipping charts*

The next best thing to a large white board is newsprint. Sheets can be mounted and turned over on an easel just like a writing pad, or posted directly on the wall. A combination usually works best. You might start writing on the easel and then, so the information remains visible, tear pages off and post them on a nearby wall. You thus create a visible record of the discussion, and it's easy to refer back to previously made points. Be selective in what you post, since displays can distract. Leave up only what helps to focus the discussion.

Paper

Flip-chart paper, also called newsprint, comes in loose sheets or in large pads. Some pads are mounted by being clamped to the easel, others by using holes along the top to fit metal rings or screws at the top of the easel. Make sure your paper fits the easel you'll be using.

Some types of paper have a grainy surface and are unmarked; other products are smooth and marked with lines one inch apart. Purists insist on un-lined paper, but if your writing has a tendency to wander and get smaller towards the edge of the paper, lines are a blessing.

Tearing sheets off a pad may look easy, but it can be tricky. A colleague suggests practicing the "matador tear": stand facing the easel, hold the sheet at the bottom left corner (if you are right-handed) and, stepping back slightly, pull away and up, cutting the sheet off at the top, along the metal clamp or the glued binding. Some pads come with a perforation that runs just below the top of the pad. Even they need practice.

If you don't want to tear off the full page, flip it over. That is why they are called flip charts. Depending on your height and reach, an elegant flipping style improves with practice. It's all part of feeling and looking confident.

Easels

Insist on an easel with a stiff (metal) backing that gives you a firm writing surface. If at all possible, work with two easels: one for the main points of the topic, the other for lists, asides, brainstorming, or keeping track of miscellaneous points. Even better are several flip charts, placed side by side across the front of the room. They make it possible to record a continuous flow of ideas as your presentation unfolds. Experiment also with easels placed in different corners of the room. Move from one to the other, redirecting attention to different angles of a topic and shifting the participants' interest around the room. Or use one or two charts for the main record and others for small-group activities involving written results.

Blank walls

If you shun the use of easels, consider working with wall-posted sheets. Begin by placing a band of tape about two inches above where you plan to post the flip-chart paper. This gives you a ready supply of tape where you need it. Keep this line of tape supplied during slow times in the meeting or at break times.

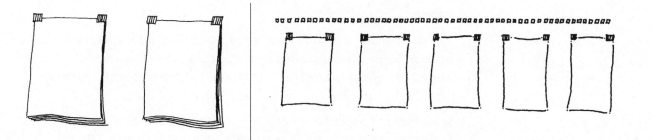

Do all this on a blank, well-lit wall. First remove all pictures and nails: keep a screwdriver and pliers in your briefcase for this purpose. Tape the sheets in five or six sections eight sheets deep; more than eight sheets tends to pull them all down. By overlapping the tape as shown above, it looks neat and well prepared. One sheet is easily removed without bringing the other sheets down. Hang sheets high enough for all to see and for you to work comfortably.

Tape

Applied carefully and removed soon after use, masking tape does not damage the walls. Seek out smooth surfaces, since walls covered with paper or textiles won't work as well. Half- to three-quarter-inch masking tape is convenient and has the sticking power – although some brands have more than others. If you use easels, cut (or neatly tear) two- to three-inch-long pieces of tape and attach them lightly to the easel legs. There they wait until you tear off a sheet and need tape to attach it to the wall.

Pens

Water-based, flat-tipped ("chisel-tip") pens work best. They do not give off the odors that make your head ache, and water-based ink on your clothes will often wash out. They also don't bleed through the sheets, whereas others can leave embarrassing marks on the wall. The chisel rather than the pointed tip makes a broad line that is easier to see. Water-based pens are available scented, a different aroma for each color. Why not?

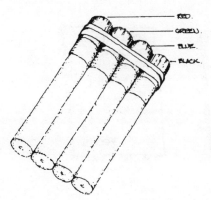

To reduce fumbling with pens and caps, make yourself a handy four-color dispenser by wrapping some masking tape around the tops as illustrated. One pen can be removed while the other three and all four caps stay taped together.

When not writing, recap and put down the pen. Holding on to pens and caps easily leads to fidgeting, which can be distracting to participants. You can also end up with messy pen marks all over your hands and clothes.

When pens run low on ink, colors fade and you hear squeaky noises when writing. The natural reaction is to put down the tired pen and reach for a fresh one. But chances are you'll pick it up again later and have to go through the rejection process all over. So, discard old pens right away.

Colors

Pens supplied with rented flip charts in hotels, schools, and training rooms usually come in one color: basic black. Come prepared with your own set and use them for the following purposes.

- Contrast: use strong colors and avoid pastels. Black and shades of green, brown, and blue are the working colors, with red reserved for emphasis. The pastels may be used effectively for underlining and circling. I'm not sure why yellow is included in the commercial packs: it is very hard to see from any distance.

- Alternate: when generating lists (during brainstorming, for instance), switch from one color to the other to distinguish one idea from the other.

- Organize: systematically use one color to label each sheet, one for topic headings, one for major points, a fourth for minor ones.

- Highlight: use circles, ovals, squares, rectangles, lines, double lines, waves, arrows, and bullets to draw attention to items on the sheet. Use symbols sparingly for maximum impact; add them as you go or to emphasize points during subsequent reviews.

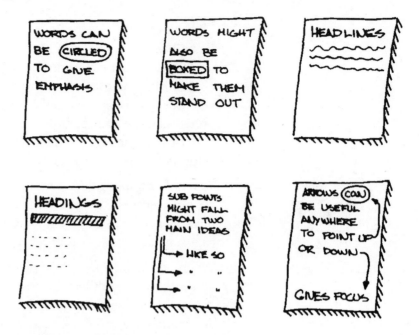

Recording techniques

If your style is anything like mine, you know that you can talk faster than you can write and that most handwritten notations are difficult to read. Experiment with the following guidelines.

- Resist the temptation to write down everything: abbreviate and condense! The idea is to capsulate an idea and record its essence.

- Print in block letters over one inch tall, even larger so that even the most distant participants can read your writing. Check occasionally to see that everyone can read it.

- Limit the entries per sheet to between eight and twelve lines; the number will depend on the size of lettering and amount of underlining and highlighting.

- Anything below table height probably can't be seen from deep in the room. To compensate for this, either leave the bottom section of the sheet blank or switch to the wall-writing technique, which allows for height adjustments.

- Write in headlines. Listen to a paragraph of words and write one line to capture the essence. Separate key thoughts from supporting ones. As participants see their words in writing, they begin to present information in recordable form – thus increasing productivity and satisfaction.

- Develop an index of abbreviations appropriate to your group and topic. My colleague David Quinlivan-Hall suggests these examples from working with business groups.[1]

+/-	plus/minus, more or less
id	identify
diff	different
w/o	without
w	with
sp	spelling
ie	that is
eg	for example
PM	participative management
EI	employee involvement
TQM	total quality management
COMP	competition
MGR	manager
EE	employee

THEREFORE	∴
GREATER	>
LESS	<
EQUALS	=
INCREASING	⟋
DECREASING	⟍
UP	↑
DOWN	↓

He also recommends symbols and diagrams which can speed up the recording function as long as your group is clear on their meaning.

Where to stand

- Don't talk to the flip chart. Write, then turn around and continue the interaction.

- Do pace your recording. When done writing, step aside and give participants a few moments to read, reflect, comment, or take notes.

- Don't block the view. If people can't see well, move the easel around or suggest participants relocate to where they can see. By the way, such an invitation offers those with hearing and seeing difficulties a gracious opening to change seats.

- Do walk around the room and look at your own handiwork from the participants' angle. If necessary, adjust your recording style and technique.

Prepared sheets

- Some charts, models, lists, and diagrams benefit from advance preparation and artistic touches. If meant for repeated use, they can be laminated for a clean appearance time after time.

- Mistakes are easily repaired. Minor ones can be fixed with white-out liquid (there's a special one for pen and ink). Larger errors can be pasted over with a piece of newsprint attached with transparent tape.

- Transport prepared sheets rolled up, in a cardboard mailing tube or, for that smart look, in a shoulder-strapped tube. People will think you are an artist – and so they should.

- Reveal the prepared posters when the time comes. Putting them up too early will divert attention from your lead-in discussion. Leaving them up too long may clutter the room and distract participants. Some posters are needed for reference and should stay posted throughout the session.

Instructional processes defined

Labels are helpful when we wish to communicate our instructional intentions. Coolie Verner proposes the following terminology for adult educators.[2]

- Methods *are ways in which a quantity of potential adult learners is organized into a structured learning event. There are individual methods such as directed study, distance education, apprenticeship, and mentored learning; and group methods as practised in workshops, seminars and classes.*

- Techniques *are the very approaches described in this book to bring teacher and learner together to accomplish a series of learning tasks.*

- Devices *are the gadgets and tools we use to support our work. They include films, projectors, video equipment, flip charts, newsprint, felt pens, models, and even the choice of facility and seating arrangements.*

27 | Showing films

Formulate your questions so they demand longish answers. By referring to areas of knowledge – rather than simple facts – you encourage more than yes and no answers.

Training films can be entertaining and provide visual stimulation. But their real value lies in supporting and expanding your instructional activities. Such use involves extra work, not less. To use films as legitimate partners in the facilitation of learning calls for thoughtful selection, prescreening, integration, and follow-through.

Use films to ...
- present alternative means of transmitting information (film may require few reading skills)
- make visible things that are too small to see with the naked eye or too large or difficult to view in person
- provide a close-up of processes and experiences, bring experts to the classroom, demonstrate complex procedures and equipment, visit out-of-the-way locations
- take advantage of frame-by-frame analysis and discussion by stopping the films at any time; films can also be shown or viewed again, either by the whole group or at individual learner's convenience

Three cautions

Outdated films quickly lose their appeal.
If the language is dated, the lapels too wide, the hairstyle too fluffy, training films lose their impact on the viewers. Preview them in their entirety to assess suitability. If in doubt, don't show.

By themselves, films are mere one-way communications.
And they assume everyone follows at the same speed and level of comprehension. Since learning styles differ from viewer to viewer, some may be bored and others overwhelmed. Create preparation and follow-up to alleviate these limitations.

Films must have a clear purpose.
Why are you showing this film or tape? How does it contribute to learning? If it is for entertainment only, say so; if it is to teach, make sure learners are ready and willing. Don't use films to fill time.

How to make the best use of films

1. Plan ahead.

- Find out what's available. Check with various sources, including the resource center of the public or college library, in-house inventory, trade and professional associations, foreign trade commissions, and government agencies. Don't trust the descriptions given by lenders and distributors. Their job is to make the product enticing and to sell or rent it.

- Determine the usefulness of the film to your particular situation. Only you can assess whether it contains the right message, is appropriate to the maturity of your group, and uses suitable examples, situations, and language. Poor acting, even dated hairstyles and lapels, will interfere with an otherwise well-written film: viewers get easily turned off and will miss the content. A poorly acted or dated film will reflect negatively on your judgment and expertise. The production quality also influences an audience's acceptance; raised on slick television and film programs, few people will tolerate poorly produced training films.

- Check whether this audience is already familiar with the film. Some people may already have seen it. Do this in advance and find out what they thought of the film. It may be possible to show it again *if* you can ensure that your context is distinct from the previous one. The techniques explained below can also help to make this quite a different viewing experience. If in doubt, don't show a repeat film.

2. Preview the film.

- If you can't preview a film, talk to someone you trust who has seen it and can provide an objective description. If only parts of the film suit your instructional goals, consider blocking those parts (by keeping track of the meter reading) and show only these segments. (Make sure the preview equipment and the one you will use in class have matching meters.)

- Determine rental costs and sources of funding. Get this sorted out in advance to avoid being stuck with the rental fee afterwards. Short rentals can run between $5 and $400 per day.

- Book the film in advance and obtain a written confirmation. Determine whether it requires delivery, pickup, and return. Ensure its arrival some time before you actually need it. This will give you time to trace its whereabouts should there be a foul-up.

When using comedy make sure that all humor arises out of the teaching points themselves so that every time the audience laughs, they're taking a point. And if they remember the joke, they've remembered the training point.

– John Cleese, the star of *Fawlty Towers* and *A Fish Called Wanda*, is the genius behind several management training films produced by Video Arts. Quoted in *Training* magazine.

- Book and inspect the projection equipment. Familiarize yourself with its operation. Check all cable connections and do a quick trial run. Whom do you call for assistance if there's a technical problem?

- Inspect the room arrangement for its suitability for viewing. Overhead lights may cause an on-screen glare, so experiment with the lighting or positioning of the monitor. Video-playback does not require blackout: it only enhances napping and makes note-taking difficult. You may be able to switch off some of the lights or relocate the monitor to somewhere other than the front of the room. You can even dramatize the film's contribution by placing the screen at the side or back of the room and asking the group to temporarily change position.

3. Prepare participants.

- Relate the film to the course content. Explain its setting and peculiarities if any, and quiz students on relevant background information. Get students to start thinking about the film in advance. Refer to vocabulary and concepts the film will use. Foreshadow the action by such comments as "The film depicts three incidents in which ..." or "Once you have seen the example in the film...." By setting up the film and bridging it with already familiar materials, you can ensure a smooth flow from in-class discussions and readings to the film and back again.

- Tell viewers what they can expect to see and learn from this film. You can lend extra depth to it by preparing and going over a handout which states the objectives, concepts, and special terminology of the film. Describe how it fits into the overall content of the course and what the learners are expected to take away from it.

- Instruct participants to look for specific problem areas illustrated in the film. For example, when viewing a management training film, one group could be asked to look specifically at nonverbal communication, while another group observes areas that relate to team building.

- Be clear if you expect learners to take notes. You may also ask them to jot down questions that arise as the action unfolds. Tell them what types of activities you have planned after the film: a discussion, a question-and-answer session, opportunity for practice, etc.

I shall the effect of this good lesson keep, As watchman to my heart.

– William Shakespeare, *Hamlet*, Act I, Scene 3.

4. Show the film.

- Avoid fumbling with mechanical details. Rehearse if necessary. You may want to stop at certain points to raise a point, elicit questions, or receive reactions regarding its content and presentation.

- Remain in the room during the entire showing – even if you have seen the film before. If you leave the room, what are you saying about the importance of the film? If you talk or cause distraction during the showing, can you expect others to give their full attention? Your behavior portrays your attitude towards the material being shown and can influence your audience's acceptance of the film.

5. Integrate the film with other activities.

- Plan to make the film's message a legitimate part of the course content. Opportunities present themselves prior to the showing, at important points during the film when you can stop the action, or at the end. If the film is controversial or has aroused strong emotions, effective questions might be "What is your reaction to that scene?" or "How do you feel about the situation you have just witnessed?" If the material is complex and apt to cause confusion, consider breaking the film into chunks interspersed with brief summaries and discussions. Identify the key concepts thus far or ask specific questions pertaining to the material.

- Be prepared to summarize key scenes, elicit lists of major points, or offer connections to previously studied material. Ask if anyone wrote down questions or wants to ask about specific issues raised by the film. Use whatever response is given to expand into a discussion that involves more than just one or two participants. If you prepared a previewing handout, use the discussion questions mentioned there to get things rolling. Ask learners to refer to specific instances in the film. Encourage them to argue with points raised in the film.

6. Follow up.

- Keep a record of the course name, the audience profile, and the film's acceptance. Note when in the proceedings you showed the film, how you introduced it, what activities followed, plus other comments to help you make good use of the film the next time around (or avoid ever using it again).

- Refer back to the film on subsequent occasions: "How did the trainer in the video approach this situation?" or "What were the three exceptions to the rule which we saw illustrated in the film?"

Adults tend to relate learning to their immediate and short-term needs. Tailor the course to learners' real-life situations.

Eight ways to integrate films

Experiment! Assign any of the following roles to individuals or small groups of three to six people. Tasks can be assigned before or after viewing. Allot between five and thirty minutes of class time.

- **Frame questions.**

  A straightforward technique is to discuss the film with the aim of generating a list of questions the film raised. Questions may be posed by small groups and responded to by individuals, other groups, or the class as a whole.

- **Specify learning.**

  Another easy way to put the group to work is to ask them to zero in on one or two important ideas that are introduced in the film. The group is challenged to think in terms of "what have we learned?"

- **Respond to specific questions.**

  Have small groups focus on specific questions raised by the film. The questions may be posted on newsprint or distributed as a handout in advance of the session. You may give each small group one or two questions of a special sort, or all small groups may work on the same question(s). Depending on the available time, the process may be repeated.

- **Brainstorm.**

  The film may introduce a problem which can be worked on in a brainstorming session. A group of six to twelve people, plus a recorder to capture the ideas, works well. You might serve as a recorder, or the recorder might be drawn from the group, depending on the number of groups at work.

- **Critique assigned readings.**

  Provide a relevant article or handout and ask for it to be discussed in relation to the film. Steer the participants away from a discussion of cinematic qualities and ask them to concentrate on the film's content.

- **Function as viewing teams.**

  Assign small groups specific viewer roles and ask them to comment on the film from their respective vantage points. For example, different subgroups are assigned one or all of the following roles.

  Questioners: "The film raises these questions for us."

  Clarifiers: "The film contradicted the text's contention that ..." or "There was some confusion regarding...."

  Dissenters: "We didn't like ..." or "We don't agree with...."

Assenters: "We respond positively to ..." or "We agree with...."

Appliers: "We can see the following applications...."

- **Assess personal effectiveness.**

  Invite participants to assess their own behavior in relation to the examples depicted in the film. For instance, for a film on team-building techniques, they could be asked to identify and discuss their own difficulties with the task of delegation. Or for a film on discrimination, they could share personal experiences with the situations depicted in the film. Both will involve self-disclosure on the part of participants and will require an atmosphere of trust.

Notes

1: On becoming a teacher

1 C. Verner, "Definition of Terms," in *Adult Education: Outlines of an Emerging Field of University Study*.

2 J. Dewey, *Democracy and Education*.

3 P. Freire, *Pedagogy of the Oppressed*.

4 K. Lewin, *Resolving Social Conflict*.

5 D.A. Kolb, *Experiential Learning, p. 21*. A comprehensive statement of the theory of experiential learning – based on the theories of Jung, Dewey, Lewin and Piaget – and applications for education, work, and lifelong development. Kolb also created the *Learning Styles Inventory* (discussed later in this book), which attempts to measure an individual's learning style in relation to the four stages of the model proposed by Lewin.

6 C.Rogers, *Freedom to Learn*.

7 M. Knowles, *The Adult Learner: A Neglected Species*, 2nd ed., ch. 3.

8 For a more systematic explanation of the behaviorist view, check any introductory psychology text, or B.F. Skinner, *Beyond Freedom and Dignity*.

9 R.Mager, *Preparing Instructional Objectives*.

10 J.E. Kemp, *The Instructional Design Process*.

11 G.O. Grow, "Teaching Learners to be Self-directed," *Adult Education Quarterly*.

12 P. Hersey and K. Blanchard, *Management of Organizational Behavior: Utilizing Human Resources*.

2: Planning a session

1 Look for reliable assistance in at least two sources: Kemp's *The Instructional Design Process*, and my own *The (Quick) Instructional Planner*.

2 For more information on the construction and application of learning objectives, consult either Mager's *Preparing Instructional Objectives,* or Gronlund's *Stating Behavioral Objectives for Classroom Instruction*.

3 R.F. Mager. *Preparing Instructional Objectives*. See also his *Goal Analysis*, *Analyzing Performance Problems* (with Peter Pipe), *Developing Attitude Toward Learning*, and *Developing Vocational Instruction* (with Kenneth M. Beach, Jr.).

5: Breaking the ice

1 Three reliable sources for warmup activities: *Warmups for Meeting Leaders* by S. Bianchi, *Saying Hello: Getting Your Group Started* by L. Hart, and *A Compendium of Icebreakers, Energizers, and Introductions* by A. Kirby.

2 D.R. Garrison and P. Brook, "Getting it Right the First Session," in *Adult Learning*.

3 Adapted from "Common Concerns Checklist," by C.H. Merman, in *Training & Development Journal*.

4 For more, see Mager's *Goal Analysis*.

5 Two books provide good details on involving participants in agenda-building: *How to Make Meetings Work* by M. Doyle and D. Strauss, and *In Search of Solutions: 60 Ways to Guide Your Problem-solving Group* by D. Quinlivan-Hall and P. Renner.

6 K.P. Cross, *Adults as Learners*, pp. 154-157.

6: Contracting for learning

1 For a rationale and guidelines for the use of learning contracts, see Knowles, *The Adult Learner: A Neglected Species*, pp. 198-203.

2 C.R. Rogers, *Client-centered Therapy*, pp. 388-391. See also *On Becoming a Person* and *Freedom to Learn* by the same author.

7: Working in groups

1 This variation was suggested by Mardy Wheeler, training director, loss prevention department, Liberty Mutual Insurance Company, Boston, MA.

2 M.E. Shaw, *Group Dynamics: The Psychology of Small Group Behavior*, pp. 185-192.

8: Delivering lively lectures

1 S. Brookfield, *The Skillful Teacher*, p. 75.

2 G.A. Brown and M.A. Bakhar (eds.), *Styles of Lecturing*.

3 R.L. Weaver, "Effective Lecturing Techniques," in *The Clearing House*.

4 M. Silberman offers excellent suggestions on lecturing in his book *Active Training*, pp. 39-77.

5 Adapted from J. Detz, *How to Write & Give a Speech*, p. 94.

6 For a summary of current humor research, see R. Zemke, "Humor in Training: Laugh and the World Learns with You – Maybe," in *Training* magazine.

7 C.R. Gruner, "Advice to the Beginning Speaker on Using Humor – What Research Tells Us," in *Communication Education*.

9: Asking beautiful questions

1 The two studies are cited in "Toward Asking the Right Questions," by R.J. Kloss, in *The Clearing House*.

2 B. Bloom (editor). *Taxonomy of Educational Objectives: Handbook I - the Cognitive Domain*.

3 "But ... do I have Time to do it Right?" by D. Schumaker in *Developing Minds: A Resource Book for Teaching Thinking*, edited by A. Costa. Cited in Kloss, above, p. 247.

4 Adapted and reproduced by permission of Training House, Inc., Princeton, NJ. See copyright page for full details.

5 "The Art of Questioning your Students," by D.M. Fairbairn in *The Clearing House*.

6 N. Postman and C. Weingartner, *Teaching as a Subversive Activity*.

10: Flexing learning styles

1 D.A. Kolb, *The Learning Style Inventory: Technical Manual*. The LSI can be completed in less than 30 minutes. To order, contact McBer & Company, 137

Newbury Street, Boston, MA 02116; telephone (800) 729-8074.

2 Another useful instrument is the *Learning Styles Questionnaire* (LSQ), developed by English psychologists Peter Honey and Alan Mumford. To order, contact Organizational Design & Development, Suite 100, 2002 Renaissance Boulevard, King of Prussia, PA 19406; telephone (215) 279-2002.

3 "The Learning Style Inventory: Still Less than Meets the Eye," by S.A. Stumpf and R.D. Friedman, in *Academy of Management Review*.

4 Kolb has written extensively on experiential learning theory and individual learning styles. A good place to start is his *Experiential Learning*.

11: Observing group behavior

1 Adapted from the classic article by K.D. Benne and P. Seats, "Functional Roles of Group Members", *Journal of Social Issues*.

2 For a fuller discussion and extensive references, see R.A. Schmuck and P.A. Schmuck. *Group Processes in the Classroom*.

3 W. Schutz, *The Interpersonal Underworld*.

14: Directing role-plays

1 N.W. Steinaker and M.R. Bell. *The Experiential Taxonomy*.

2 A. Mehrabian, *Silent Messages*.

3 E.T. Hall, *The Hidden Dimension*, and *The Silent Language*.

15: Teaching by demonstration

1 O.A. Spaid, *The Consumate Trainer: A Practitioner's Perspective*, p. 156.

2 R.C. Clark, *Developing Technical Training*.

3 The 1981 film *You'll Soon Get the Hang of It* expertly shows how to conduct on-the-job training. It is produced by Video Arts Limited.

4 R.M. Gagné, *The Conditions of Learning*.

16: Inspiring participation

1 C.R. Rogers, *Freedom to Learn*, pp. 164-166.

17: Studying cases

1 Adapted from "Making Case Studies Come Alive," by P.H. Owenby, in *Training* magazine.

20: Individualizing assignments

1 Adapted from D.W. Johnson and F.P. Johnson, *Joining Together* 3rd ed., p.17, which draws on Lewin's classic, "Dynamics of Group Action."

21: Writing in journals

1 Based on "Journal as Dialogue," by J. Zimmerman, in *Synergist* magazine.

2 Based on "Journal as Discipline," by C. Norman, in *Synergist* magazine.

3 Reported by L. McAlpine in "Learning to Reflect: Using Journals as Professional Conversations," in *Adult Learning*.

22: Assessing the course

1 R.M. Gagné, "Domains of Learning," in *Interchange*.

23: Giving and receiving feedback

1 Adapted from "Making Feedback Work," by J.A. Raelin, in *Training & Development Journal*.

24: Designing tests and quizes

1 M. Knowles, *The Making of an Adult Educator*.

2 S. Brookfield, "Giving Helpful Evaluations to Learners," in *Adult Learning*. I highly recommend *The Skillful Teacher* by the same author.

3 Adapted from "Beyond Evaluation Myths," by M.Q. Patton, in *Adult Learning*.

4 M.Q. Patton, "Beyond Evaluation Myths," in *Adult Learning*, p. 28.

5 For more information, consult the following texts. N.E. Gronlund, *How to Construct Achievement Tests*; J.E. Kemp, *The Instructional Design Process* (chapter 11); R.F Mager, *Measuring Instructional Results*; M.Q. Patton, *Utilization-Focused Evaluation*; R.L. Thorndike and E. Hagen, *Measurement and Evaluation in Psychology and Education*; D.L. Stufflebeam, *Systematic Evaluation*.

6 Based on N.E. Gronlund, *How to Construct Achievement Tests*, pp. 30-43. Check in your library for the most recent edition.

7 N.E. Gronlund, *How to Construct Achievement Tests*, pp. 45-46.

8 N.E. Gronlund, *How to Construct Achievement Tests*, pp. 49-50.

9 M. Priestley, *Performance Assessment in Education & Training: Alternative Techniques*, p. 195.

10 Briefly summarized in "Essay Tests: Use, Development, and Grading," by A.C. Ornstein, in *The Clearing House*.

11 S. Brookfield, *The Skillful Teacher*, p. 22.

12 A.C. Ornstein, "Essay Tests," pp. 176-177.

25: Projecting overhead

1 M. Knowles. *The Adult Learner*, p. 31.

26: Flipping charts

1 D. Quinlivan-Hall is co-author of *In Search of Solutions*. The illustrations on pp. 120-123 are taken from that book and were prepared by Bradley McTavish.

2 C. Verner and A. Booth, in *Adult Education*.

Bibliography

Bach, Richard. *Illusions: The Adventures of a Reluctant Messiah.* New York: Dell Publishing, 1977.

Benne, K.D., and P. Seats. "Functional Roles of Group Members." *Journal of Social Issues* 4(1948):41-49.

Bianchi, Susan, and Jan Butler. *Warmups for Meeting Leaders.* San Diego, CA: Pfeiffer & Company, 1984.

Bloom, Benjamin, ed. *Taxonomy of Educational Objectives: Handbook I - the Cognitive Domain.* New York: McKay, 1956.

Blum, Robert. *The Book of Runes.* New York: St. Martin's Press, 1987.

Brookfield, Stephen. "Giving Helpful Evaluations to Learners." *Adult Learning* June 1992, p. 22.

——. *The Skillful Teacher.* San Francisco: Jossey-Bass, 1991.

Brown, G.A., and M.A. Bakhar, eds. *Styles of Lecturing.* Loughborough, England: Loughborough University Press, 1983.

Clark, Ruth C. *Developing Technical Training.* Reading, MA: Addison-Wesley, 1989.

Cross, K. Patricia. *Adults as Learners.* San Francisco: Jossey-Bass, 1981.

Detz, Joan. *How to Write & Give a Speech.* New York: St. Martin's Press, 1984 (revised 1992).

Dewey, John. *Democracy and Education: An Introduction to the Philosophy of Education.* New York: Macmillan, 1916.

——. *Experience and Education.* New York: Collier, 1963.

Didion, Joan. "On Keeping a Notebook." In *Slouching Towards Bethlehem.* New York: Dell, 1968.

Doyle, Michael, and David Strauss. *How to Make Meetings Work.* New York: Jove Pubns., 1986.

Fairbairn, D.M. "The Art of Questioning your Students." *The Clearing House,* September 1987, pp. 19-22.

Freire, Paulo. *Pedagogy of the Oppressed.* New York: Seabury Press, 1973.

Gagné, Robert M. *The Conditions of Learning.* 3rd ed. New York: Holt-Reinhart-Winston, 1977 (revised 1985).

——. "Domains of Learning." *Interchange* 3:1-8.

Garrison, D. Randy, and Paula Brook. "Getting it Right the First Session." *Adult Learning*, August 1992, pp. 25-26.

Gerard, R.W. "The Biology of the Imagination." In *The Creative Process*, Brewster Ghiselin, ed. New York: Mentor, 1952.

Gronlund, Norman. *How to Construct Achievement Tests*. Englewood Cliffs, NJ: Prentice-Hall, 1968 (revised 1987).

——. *How to Write Instructional Objectives*. New York: Free Press, 1990.

——. *Stating Behavioral Objectives for Classroom Instruction*. Englewood Cliffs, NJ: Prentice-Hall, 1968.

Grow, Gerald O. "Teaching Learners to be Self-directed." *Adult Education Quarterly* 41:125-149.

Gruner, C.R. "Advice to the Beginning Speaker on Using Humor – What Research Tells Us." *Communication Education* 34(2):142-47.

Hall, Edward T. *The Hidden Dimension*. New York: Doubleday, 1966.

——. *The Silent Language*. New York: Doubleday, 1971.

Hart, Lois. *Saying Hello: Getting Your Group Started*. 2nd ed. King of Prussia, PA: Organizational Design & Development, 1989.

Hersey, Paul, and Ken Blanchard. *Management of Organizational Behavior: Utilizing Human Resources*. 5th ed. Englewood Cliffs, NJ: Prentice-Hall, 1988.

Johnson, David, and Frank Johnson. *Joining Together*. 3rd ed. Englewood Cliffs, NJ: Prentice-Hall, 1987.

Kemp, Jerrold E. *The Instructional Design Process*. New York: HarperCollins, 1990.

Kirby, Andy. *A Compendium of Icebreakers, Energizers, and Introductions*. Amherst, MA: Human Resource Development Press, 1992.

Kloss, R.J. "Toward Asking the Right Questions." *The Clearing House*, February 1988, pp. 245-248.

Knowles, Malcolm. *The Adult Learner: A Neglected Species*. 2nd ed. Houston, TX: Gulf Publishing Company, 1978.

——. *The Making of an Adult Educator*. San Francisco: Jossey-Bass, 1989.

Kolb, David A. *Experiential Learning: Experience as the Source of Learning and Development*. Englewood Cliffs, NJ: Prentice-Hall, 1984.

——. *The Learning Style Inventory: Technical Manual*. Boston: McBer & Company, 1976 (revised 1985).

Lao Tzu, *Tao Te Ching*. Translated by Stephen Mitchell, New York: HarperCollins Publishers, 1988.

Lao Tzu, *Tao Teh Ching*. Translated by John C.H. Wu. New York: St. John's University Press, 1961.

Lewin, Kurt. "Dynamics of Group Action." *Educational Leadership* 1:195-200.

——. *Resolving Social Conflict: Selected Papers on Group Discussion*. New York: Harper, 1948.

Mager, Robert. *Developing Attitude Toward Learning*. Belmont, CA: Fearon-Pitman Publishers, 1984.

———. *Goal Analysis*. Belmont, CA: Fearon, 1972 (revised 1984).

———. *Making Instruction Work*. Belmont, CA: Lake Publishing Co., 1988.

———. *Measuring Individual Results*. Belmont, CA: Lake Publishing Co., 1984.

———. *Preparing Instructional Objectives*. 2nd ed. Belmont, CA: Lake Publishing Co., 1984.

Mager, Robert, and Kenneth M. Beach, Jr. *Developing Vocational Instruction*. Belmont, CA: Fearon-Pitman Publishers, 1967.

Mager, Robert, and Peter Pipe. *Analyzing Performance Problems*. Belmont, CA: Fearon-Pitman Publishers, 1984.

Mathieu, W.A. *The Listening Book: Discovering Your Own Music*. Boston: Shambhala, 1991.

Mayeroff, Milton. *On Caring*. New York: Harper & Row, 1971.

McAlpine, Lynn. "Learning to Reflect: Using Journals as Professional Conversations." *Adult Learning*, January 1992, pp. 15-24.

Mehrabian, Albert. *Silent Messages*. Belmont, CA: Wadsworth, 1971.

Merman, C.H. "Common Concerns Checklist." *Training & Development*, January 1992, p. 70.

Nielson, Carolyn. *Training Program Workbook & Kit*. Englewood Cliffs, NJ: Prentice-Hall, 1989.

Nin, Anaïs. *The Diary of Anaïs Nin*. Vol. V. New York: Harcourt Brace, 1964.

Norman, Charles. "Journal as Discipline." *Synergist*, Fall 1981, pp. 46-49.

Ogilvy, David. *Confessions of an Advertising Man*. New York: Ballantine, 1974.

Ornstein, A. "Essay Tests: Use, Development, and Grading." *The Clearing House*, January/February 1992, pp. 175-177.

Owenby, P.H. "Making Case Studies Come Alive." *Training*, January 1992, pp. 43-44.

Parry, Scott. "Questions About Questions." *Training & Development Journal*, February 1991.

Patton, Michael Quinn. "Beyond Evaluation Myths." *Adult Learning*, October 1991, pp. 9-28.

———. *Utilization-Focused Evaluation*. Newbury Park, CA: Sage Pubns., 1986.

Postman, Neil, and Charles Weingartner. *Teaching as a Subversive Activity*. New York: Delta Books, 1969.

Priestley, M. *Performance Assessment in Education & Training: Alternative Techniques*. Englewood Cliffs, NJ: Educational Technology Publications, 1982.

Quinlivan-Hall, David, and Peter Renner. *In Search of Solutions: Sixty Ways to Guide Your Problem-Solving Group*. Vancouver, BC: Training Associates, 1990.

Raelin, J.A. "Making Feedback Work." *Training & Development Journal*, July 1989, p. 25.

Reiss, C.R. "Turning Technicians into Trainers." *Training*, July 1991, pp. 47-50.

Renner, Peter. *The Instructor's Survival Kit: A Handbook for Teachers of Adults*. 2nd ed. Vancouver, BC: Training Associates, 1983.

——. *The (Quick) Instructional Planner*. Vancouver, BC: Training Associates, 1988.

Rogers, Carl R. *Client-centered Therapy*. Boston: Houghton-Mifflin, 1951.

——. *Freedom to Learn: A View of What Education Might Become*. Columbus, OH: Merrill, 1969.

——. *On Becoming a Person*. Boston: Houghton-Mifflin, 1961.

Schmuck, Richard, and Patricia Schmuck. *Group Processes in the Classroom*. Dubuque, IA: Wm. C. Brown, 1971 (revised 1992).

Schumaker, D. "But ... do I have Time to do it Right?" In *Developing Minds: A Resource Book for Teaching Thinking* edited by A. Costa. Alexandria, VA: Association for Supervision and Curriculum Development, 1985.

Schutz, Will. *The Interpersonal Underworld*. Palo Alto, CA: Science & Behavior Books, 1966.

Sellar, Walter Carruthers, and Robert Julian Yeatman. *1066 and all that. A Memorable History of England, comprising all the parts you can remember, including 103 Good Things, 5 Bad Kings and 2 Genuine Dates*. London: Methuen & Co., 1930 (Reissued by Mandarin Paperbacks, 1991).

Sentsan. *hsin hsin ming*. Translated by Richard B. Clarke. Buffalo, NY: White Pine Press, 1984.

Shaw, Marvin. *Group Dynamics: The Psychology of Small Group Behavior*. New York: McGraw Hill, 1976 (revised 1980).

Silberman, Mel. *Active Training: A Handbook of Techniques, Designs, Case Examples, and Tips*. San Diego, CA: Pfeiffer & Company, 1990.

Skinner, B.F. *Beyond Freedom and Dignity*. New York: Alfred Knopf, 1971.

Spaid, Ora A. *The Consumate Trainer: A Practitioner's Perspective*. Englewood Cliffs, NJ: Prentice-Hall, 1986.

Steinaker, N.W., and M.R. Bell. *The Experiential Taxonomy*. New York: Academic Press, 1979.

Stufflebeam, Daniel L. *Systematic Evaluation*. Norwell, MA: Kluwer, 1984.

Stumpf, S.A., and R.D. Friedman. "The Learning Style Inventory: Still Less than Meets the Eye." *Academy of Management Review* 6(2):297-299.

Thorndike, Robert L., and Elizabth P. Hagen. *Measurement and Evaluation in Psychology and Education*. New York: Macmillan, 1977.

Verner, Coolie. "Definition of Terms." In *Adult Education: Outlines of an Emerging Field of University Study* edited by G. Jensen, A.A. Liveright, and W.C. Hallenbeck. Washington, DC: Adult Education Association of America, 1964.

Verner, Coolie, and A. Booth. *Adult Education*. New York: Center for Applied Research in Education, 1964.

von Oech, Roger. *A Whack on the Side of the Head: How to Unlock Your Mind for Innovation*. New York: Warner Books, 1983 (revised 1990).

Weaver, R.L. "Effective Lecturing Techniques." *The Clearing House* 55(1):20-33.

Zemke, Ron. "Humor in Training: Laugh and the World Learns with You – Maybe." *Training*, August 1991, pp. 26-29.

Zimmerman, Jane. "Journal as Dialogue." *Synergist* (Fall 1981):46-49.

Index

Related titles

In Search of Solutions: Sixty Ways to Guide Your Problem-Solving Group
by David Quinlivan-Hall & Peter Renner

A step-by-step guide to cultivating your skills at chairing meetings, leading committees, or working with just about any problem-solving group. Two experienced facilitators explain how and when to apply over sixty intervention techniques. With their assistance, you learn to guide your team through the critical phases of problem-solving to define the issues, identify the "real" problem, generate ideas, make decisions, and plan for action.
144 pages, 6x9" paperback
ISBN 0-9690465-8-8
CAN$ 27 / US$ 25

The (Quick) Instructional Planner
by Peter Renner

This workbook shows content experts how to plan courses, workshops, or presentations. Packed with straightforward steps to determine where to start, what to include, how to generate ideas, how to sequence events, which teaching techniques to use, and how to evaluate. Full of examples, checklists and tricks-of-the-trade. You may copy the worksheets over and over.
121 pages, 8.5x10" paperback
ISBN 0-9690465-6-1
CAN$ 27 / US$ 25

The Art of Teaching Adults
by Peter Renner
151 pages, 8.5x10"
paperback CAN$ 28 / US$ 26
ISBN 0-9697319-0-6;
hardcover CAN$ 36 / US$ 32
ISBN 0-9060465-9-6

Payment
Orders *must be prepaid* by check/ cheque, VISA or Mastercard. We'll invoice repeat and quantity orders as soon as we receive your official Purchase Order by fax or mail.

Shipping Costs
Add $4.00 for the first book *plus* $1.50 for every additional. Canadian customers add 7% GST to the total bill (book + shipping charge + GST).

Shipping
We attempt to ship every order within three working days of receipt. For regular delivery by post, allow 2 to 6 weeks.

Rush orders
We are unable to ship small orders by UPS since the U.S. Customs brokerage charge of up to $25 per order makes this a very expensive proposition. For quantity UPS orders, please phone for a quote. If you wish, however, we'll ship any item C.O.D. by the courier of your choice.

Discounts
10–40 books = 10%
41– 80 books = 15%
81–120 books = 20%
Bookstores & Distributors receive a 20% discount on *prepaid* orders, for any quantity.

Three quick ways to order
1. *Phone* your order to 604-732-4552 between 9 am and 5 pm Pacific Time. We accept VISA or Mastercard.
2. *Fax* your order to 604-738-4080 at any time.
3. *Mail* your order on official stationary or purchase order form to Training Associates, Suite 720, 999 West Broadway, Vancouver, BC V5Z 1K5 Canada.

Our unconditional guarantee
You will receive a refund of the book price for any item returned in resale condition within 30 days.

Order Form

Training Associates
#720 - 999 West Broadway
Vancouver, BC
V5Z 1K5 Canada

Tel (604) 732-4552
Fax (604) 738-4080

Shipping costs

In Canada:
$4 for the first book + $1.50 for each additional item. Add 7% GST to the total bill (book + shipping + tax).

To the USA:
$4 for the first book + $1.50 for each additional title.

Bookstores and distributors receive a 20% discount on **prepaid** orders, regardless of quantity.

Please send me

Quantity	Title	US$	Can$	Total
	The Art of Teaching Adults (paperback)	26	28	
	The Art of Teaching Adults (hardcover)	32	36	
	The (Quick) Instructional Planner	25	27	
	In Search of Solutions	25	27	

Add shipping cost $ _____

Subtotal $ _____

Canadian customers, **add** 7% GST to the Subtotal $ _____

Grand Total $ _____

Your Day-Time Telephone (___) ___ - _____

Your Fax Number (___) ___ - _____

Choice of payment: ☐ Cheque ☐ VISA ☐ MasterCard

Name on credit card _____

Card Number _____

Expiry date ___ / ___

Your Signature _____

Ship to

Name _____

Title _____

Department _____

Company _____

Address _____

_____

City _____

State/Province _____

Zip/Postal Code _____

Prices are guaranteed until June 30, 1998.